Self-Love
Boot Camp

Letters to a young mystic

J A C O B   G L A S S

ISBN-10: 1523203617
ISBN-13: 978-1523203611

PREFACE AND DEDICATION

This book is dedicated to my 17 year-old self and to young mystics of all ages. I consider this a trip through an inter-dimensional portal that glides along the corridors of time to deliver to my younger self the mentoring I needed at that time. In my mind I imagine that it fell off a bookshelf in a library or bookstore, or that I found it in a cave in rural Pennsylvania where I grew up – and that it is a handbook for learning how to love and accept myself (and you to love your self) in a world where I was systematically taught from birth to hate and judge myself – by the culture, the church, the advertisers and media, by the world at large. Most of us are taught this in one way or another.

This is a daily boot camp for neutralizing all that self-loathing to replace it with love and self-acceptance. It is what I have learned so far as a modern mystic living in America in the technological age. It is encouragement and guidance to my younger self when it would have most shifted my Consciousness and avoided a lot of pain. However, I do not regret any of that pain because it brought me to the place where I am able to help others help themselves now. This book is one of those ways.

Perhaps you will find it helpful too. But be warned that it is politically incorrect, probably has spelling and grammar errors and uses very adult language at times. It may outrage you, or it may set you free – that's up to you. This book started as a blog which hundreds of people read every day, so it's written to my 17 year-old self and to all those who showed up at the blog every day. Suffice to say, a lot of lives were radically changed in very positive ways and I am very thankful for that.

Please do not think of self-love as an emotion or feeling of affection. That is only one small aspect of self-love. Real love is an ACTION – it is something that we DO. We cannot depend on our ever-changing emotions and moods when it comes to love. A mother may not always FEEL loving affectionate feelings for a toddler who has just thrown a tantrum at the mall and destroyed and entire display while making a huge scene. But she doesn't refuse to feed him that day or tell him to find his own way home from the store. And yet, many of us abandon and punish ourselves on a daily basis for far smaller reasons.

This is why it's a self-love BOOT CAMP of taking action – whether we "feel like it" or not! It is the absolute refusal to abandon ourselves for any reason. It is ACTING like we love ourselves even when our "feelings" are the extreme opposite at the moment. This is learning how to rationally see our mistakes as something to be owned up to and gently corrected and learned from rather than a reason for punishment and self-loathing. It is also about turning DOWN the volume on the critical voices of the world and TURNING UP the inner voice of encouragement, approval and acceptance. THIS is the time that you do not give up on yourself. This is the time when you become your own greatest cheerleader instead of your own worst critic. It's the time when you take total responsibility for getting on your own team instead of joining the invisible opposition. This is it. You're as ready as you're ever going to be – start today. You can do this. It's easier than you think.

No one can
give to you
what you are
unwilling to give
to yourself.

EPIGRAPH

"These roses under my window make no reference to former roses or better ones; they are for what they are; they exist with God to-day. There is no time to them. There is simply the rose; it is perfect in every moment of its existence."
- Ralph Waldo Emerson

You
Have
Something
Valuable
to
Contribute.

Acknowledgments

A huge thank you to everyone who read the Self-love Boot Camp blog and sent me encouragement to keep writing – and a lot of gratitude to Reverend Terry Cole-Whittaker who told the world *"What You Think of Me is None of My Business"* those many years ago.

Day 1 - Meet Your Team
An Introduction to Self-love Boot Camp

Welcome fellow Mystic. This is the start of your journey to owning who and what you are by stepping more fully into your life without the shackles of shame, guilt, and self-doubt. It's time for you to run free like the wild wonderful Cosmic Creation that you are so that you can fulfill your Divine Destiny in this world and beyond. Much of what you will learn in this next 90 days will fly in the face of everything that you have ever been taught in this world. It may rock your world and blow your mind. Good. It's meant to. You've been taught a lot of bullshit that is making you suffer needlessly. So, let's get started.

If we are going to practice loving our self, then that means all the various aspects of that self. To me, there are 4 pillars of our beingness: **body, mind, spirit and heart**. If we disown or ignore any of those team members, then we are not fully in the experience of self-love and we will have problems with a very lopsided self. In boot camp, we don't leave a team member behind; we don't abandon them just because we have an issue with them. We're in this together and we are most successful when all four team members have a common goal and are going in the same direction. And let me remind us all again, that love is a DOING, it is an ACTION. This may be a big challenge for you for the next 90 days, but I know that you can do it.

And please remember it is YOUR boot camp and YOU get to make it up the way it works for YOU, so don't think you have to be overwhelmed or working on all four areas every day!! What can be VERY helpful is to do one thing per week for each team member. Or perhaps 3 of the areas are very good in your life and you'll only be working on one, or you want to work on them all but it's too much to do all at one time so you are focusing on just one for now, so maybe you'll want to do something daily or 3 times a week or whatever for THAT particular member of your team. Make it up so that it is FUN and FRUITFUL for YOU! NO ONE is looking over your shoulder or judging and evaluating how you are doing. Fuck that shit. This is for YOU.

THE BODY

In the book "Life Loves You, authors Louise L. Hay and Robert Holden discuss watching toddlers and little children have their first experiences of seeing themselves in the mirror - particularly kissing their reflection over and over again - all with wild abandon and no sense of shame or guilt about it even in a room full of other people! This is the joy of life before we become "self-conscious" and start to care what others think about us more than we care about what WE think about ourselves.

So, how is your relationship with your body currently? For some of you it may be fabulous and there is very little work to do there. For others, this is the perfect time to up your body love game. Try to have fun with this rather than making it a chore. You might even want to push yourself to kiss yourself in the mirror first thing in the morning saying, *"Hello dear friend, I'm so happy to see you again cause you are getting more fucking adorable every day!"*

2

How are you treating your body? Just consider, WITHOUT BLAME OR GUILT, what you are eating, how you are exercising or not, if you are treating it with tenderness with massage even if it is self-massage, if you are judging it, or resisting some condition it has, and so on. Then, decide if there are changes you want to make during this 90-day boot camp - and begin making them, TODAY. Remember, we don't *"whip into shape"* a beloved friend who is a member of our team. We want this to be a challenge, but one filled with encouragement, kindness, love and patience, not bullying. And since we take our bodies with us almost everywhere we go, this is as good a time as any to make peace with it and see it clearly instead of through the filter of the insane culture of the Western world. IF physical exercise is something you feel guided to do, remember that even if you have many physical limitations, there is exercise for almost everyone, like the show "Sit and Be Fit" that is often on public television.

Affirmation: *My body is my oldest dearest most cherished physical friend. I'm in the process of loving my body more than ever before and it shows in the way I treat it and speak to and about it.*

THE MIND

First, let's remember that your mind is not your brain. Mind uses the organ of the brain, but mind is much more expansive than the physical organ of the brain. They work together and we want to love and appreciate both as a magnificent part of the team! Often spiritual types want to do a "bypass" of the mind and not deal with it at all. Some spiritualities demonize the mind in various ways calling it the "monkey mind" and so on - something wild that will be giving us trouble til the day we die. But mind is a dear precious friend and member of the team. It is as precious as a little puppy that needs training and then becomes like the most loyal beloved family dog who protects, and loves, and gives unconditional love, all while maintaining a keen intuitive sense and ability to "smell out" whether to trust someone new, to tune in and know what is on the way, and oh so much more!

The very first physical friend we have in this world is our own body. Babies already love their bodies and are fascinated by it though they can get very frustrated in learning just how to use it. Unfortunately many of us lose the self-love but don't lose the frustration. We can get frustrated that the body isn't doing what we want - it's in pain, it doesn't work "perfectly," it's too big or too small, it isn't stable, it's getting old, wrinkly and saggy, it has chronic conditions, is "disabled" in some way, or it was abused in the past, has scars, carries shame and so on. We don't see it as a precious unique team member that needs to be encouraged, celebrated and not compared with the bodies of other people.

How do you think of and treat your mind? A mind needs both challenge and rest - times of great activity and times of quiet and contemplation. Maybe you can begin to think of your mind as a big loving SMART loyal dog with many talents and tricks. You don't beat the dog up when it forgets or makes a mistake, nor would you withdraw your love as the dog ages and slows down in some ways. Remember, YOU CAN TEACH AN OLD DOG NEW TRICKS! With God-Source, ALL things are possible. Do NOT argue for your limitations!

So, how are you treating your mind these days? Are you allowing it to ruminate on worry and fear? Are you giving it positive challenges to keep it active the way that some people like to do crossword puzzles and such? Do you need to have a daily practice of sitting and quieting your mind for 10 minutes a day, or to have an activity that calms the mind like gardening or running, or whatever works for you? One of the things that has MOST helped me with training my mind has been filling out the daily pages from my Happiness Boot camp (which you can find at jacobglass.com) - it helps me to start my mind off every day on the right foot and going in the right direction.

Affirmation: *My mind is a wonderful constant companion, full of love and wisdom and good intuition. I am in the process of honoring my beautiful brilliant mind.*

THE SPIRIT

For our purposes here, let's consider spirit the larger expanded oceanic self that is at one with the Divine Mind and one with all of Life. Only YOU know what feeds your spirit. For a vast majority of people nature feeds their spirit very deeply. For me, it is looking out at the purple mountains of Palm Springs every day. For others, it is seeing the ocean, or their garden, or spending time with animals. Some people's spirit is fed through ritual, or community, or great art, or tai chi, or yoga, or chanting, or singing, or a meditative practice, or having bodywork. For many people, their spirit is fed by giving to others, helping, doing charity work, and visiting people who are sick and so on. One way my spirit is fed is by teaching and writing. It's very individual and most of us are fed by various ways and means. So, what feeds your spirit and have you been giving it regular nourishment? Boot camp is a wonderful time to explore various ways to feed our spirit as an ACT of self-love.

Too often we make a big "to do" about feeding our spirit and make up pedantic limiting ridiculous rules that it's going to take a long time to do it because we need to find a weekend when we can drive to the mountains, or if we can't meditate for a full half hour there's not use in doing it at all, or that we have to find exactly the right spiritual group to join, or that blah blah blah. It really is so much simpler than all of that, but we can MAKE it hard through our resistance. Much of boot camp is about RELAXING OUR RESISTANCE and increasing our willingness – allowing things to be easier as we get out of our own way.

Affirmation: *I have a beautiful spirit that I love to feed and nurture in the ways that I find most satisfying. I am in the process of expanding my appreciation for the wonderful spirit that I am.*

THE HEART

Oh my, the wonderful, wonderful heart. The heart is the feeling center of course. It is quite easy to begin to shut down our hearts as we get older because of past hurts. We may get frightened and think we are protecting our feelings by building walls around the heart, but this is another example of faulty problem solving. In many ways, it is the heart that gives MEANING to our lives, so without having it fully activated we can start to gradually move into listlessness and even depression.

This is why in my guided meditations at the start of class I ask people, *"What makes your heart sing?"* so that we can get the heart activated. Love and joy are basically the same vibration, but so often we associate the heart with wounds, weakness and sorrows. This is backward and isolationist thinking. It is the heart that usually draws us TOWARD - in fact that is so common we call it "our heart's desire." Are you allowing yourself to move TOWARD your heart's desire? It is a RADICAL act of self-love to go in the direction of your heart's desire! Motherfucking radical!!

THIS is where the rubber meets the road for many of us. It's so easy to say, *"All things are possible"* but really be thinking, *"that is if you are a good looking athletic white male 22 years old, living in America with loving educated prosperous parents and in perfect health."* But if we are an adopted 67 year old, dyslexic, multi-racial lesbian, without a high school diploma suffering from chronic migraines, we can think that the cards are stacked against us and it's too late for us to move in the direction of our heart's desire. We can reject ourselves before anyone else has a chance to. We can decide to just sit it out the rest of our lives and settle for whatever crumbs we can get by on in life. This is when we have to start to gather up the evidence of people who ARE going for it in spite of the story of their obstacles. The world is not going to try to inspire or lift us up – it is NOT going to encourage us. It will try to terrify us instead, if we allow it – if we give in.

Please don't be offended by this, but I think the word heartbreak is a drama queen term and ought to be done away with forever. Yes, our hearts FEEL broken, but it's actually wounded and sometimes terribly terribly bruised. It may be poetic to say broken, shattered, and so on, but it is not HELPFUL. Healing is a natural function of the Universe. In fact, most hearts would heal on their own if we did not keep picking at the wound or start guarding and walling it off. It is in gradually USING the heart again that it begins to gain back strength and vitality. I so admire people who do not let life's disappointments and losses put them permanently on the bench. When Elizabeth Taylor kept getting married over and over again, I couldn't help thinking, "Atta girl!" simply because she seemed to really like being married, or at least getting married. Remember, the world is going to have an opinion about whatever you do – if you are going to let that stop or inhibit you from living as you choose, you're already dead in the water.

So whether your heart's desire is to have a child, get married even though you are 80, make some new friends, enter a new exciting profession at 70 years of age, get closer to your family, or whatever, I encourage us all to take this 90 day boot camp as the perfect time to start moving out of that old comfort zone and start taking some calculated risks. I'm not talking about foolish throwing ourselves off a cliff and thinking the net will appear. We're not reckless with our team members but we don't permanently bench them either. What makes your heart sing? What is your heart's desire? If you don't know, THIS is the time to start exploring again.

Affirmation: *My heart is opening like a flower in the morning sun and I am in the process of allowing myself to feel more love and joy than ever before!*

So dear boot campers, this is our beginning. Most of our daily entries will be far shorter than this now that we have an understanding that self-love is an ACTION and you can begin to look to see where you want to put your efforts and attention!

The fun is just getting started and you are going to LOVE this process.

DAY 2 - BEGIN WITH THE END IN MIND

It's important not to simply have set the goals of your Self-love Boot Camp, but also to spend time visioning and imagining yourself as you will be when you are living those goals consistently - whether it is 90 days of eating well, doing affirmations, getting more rest, putting yourself out there in relationships, doing positive self-talk, doing yoga, spending more time in nature, or whatever. Having a VISION of yourself is going to make a huge difference in your journey and in the energy that you are summoning from the Universe and from within yourself. It is not enough to have the will to get there - we must also have IMAGINATION. When we combine will with imagination we are Imagineers practicing Visioneering. I am using ACTION words here as we keep within our theme that self-love is an ACTION.

In the 7 Habits of Highly Effective People, Stephen Covey calls this habit "Begin With the End in Mind." One of my all-time favorite New Thought teachers Neville Goddard taught something that I call "Congratulations scenes" in which you imagine someone you know looking you in the eyes and shaking your hand, or high-fiving you, or hugging you while they say "CONGRATULATIONS!" (about whatever it is that you want to have accomplished or attained) and I've had wonderful success with those at times. It's very fun. So, look to see the approximate date that you will complete our 90-day boot camp, and then IMAGINE yourself on that day and actually PUT YOURSELF THERE rather than seeing it like on a movie screen. Close your eyes and be in the scene - how do you FEEL? How do you feel in your body and in your life? What is the state of your mind, body, spirit and heart? In the scene you may want to walk over to a mirror and see yourself - how is your posture, your energy, the light in your eyes? And at some point in this BRIEF scenario (keep this brief) see the face or faces of loved ones congratulating or acknowledging you in some way for the positive changes you've made in the past 90 days, whether they are saying you seem so much more happy, or serene, or confident, or emotionally available, or stronger, or joyful, or if they are congratulating you on some action you've taken or something you've achieved - whatever it is for you.

Hold the vision before you every day as we go through this boot camp together. And remember, it's YOUR vision, not the vision society or the culture has for you, it's YOURS. Make it the way that feels right for YOU. Play with the vision - make it fun and joyful.

Another process that we've had great success in my classes with is the "letter to Jacob" process. You simply write me a letter (do not mail it) dated on the day you'll complete boot camp, joyfully telling me all the wonderful things that happened during the 90-day boot camp. Then, you read that letter to yourself every day. It's a very GENERAL letter since you don't have any idea HOW things will unfold - this process isn't about the how, it's about activating and amplifying the feelings of having already arrived at the state of Consciousness that is your goal.

There is a quote from Corinthians that is read at many weddings that I think can be helpful as a kind of self-love template which you may want to use and adapt for yourself during our boot camp - in particular *"love is patient, love is kind, it keeps no record of wrongs"* is a very empowering way to be with yourself during these 90 days. Be patient and kind with yourself, and do not keep a record of any mistakes you make along the way or become angry with yourself. If we're not falling down a little along the way it's usually because we haven't gotten off the couch. Remember to GET and STAY ON YOUR OWN TEAM!

DAY 3 - GOING IN THE RIGHT DIRECTION

One of the most unloving things that we can do is terrify ourselves with fearful and stressful thoughts and stories. Can you imagine waking up a small child in the middle of the night and talking to her endlessly about the most worrisome things you can dream up? That would not be very loving or kind. And yet many of us have done this to ourselves - imagining the very worst all night long while we toss and turn. What we want to use our beautiful Divine Imagination for is the opposite of this by imagining the best, making the best of things rather than the worst of them. It does take discipline and practice, but again, this is boot camp.

This is one of the reasons that on my daily sheet I make a lists of "Where I Got It Right" and "What Went Right" - to counteract any tendency I may have to focus on what went wrong, what could go wrong, where I got it wrong, where I am or could get it wrong. Boot camp is about letting go of any habits and tendencies to focus on flaws and instead, begin to focus and build on strengths. Remember, the way to let go of negative habits is simply to replace them with positive habits.

Focus more on simply going in the right direction than on moving faster or covering more ground. At this point, consistency in creating good habits is the most helpful and important things, so learn to soothe and encourage yourself as soon as you realize you've been scaring yourself again.

Day 4 - It's Okay, It's Okay, It's Okay

Take a nice deep breath; let your shoulders drop as you relax the jaw and all the muscles of the face and neck. Allow all tension or stress to drain out of you like sand falling through an hourglass as you quietly tell yourself, *"it's okay, it's okay, it's okay."*

I heard this on the background of a subliminal recording several years ago. Usually you cannot hear the subliminal suggestions of course, but for some reason I could hear over and over again in both a male and female voice, *"it's okay, it's okay, it's okay"* - and I cannot tell you how soothing and empowering it is to marinate in those words like an endless mantra on a loop.

Too often we bully ourselves with our thoughts that it may NOT be okay, that we are not okay, that life is not okay, that our loved ones are not okay, that the world is not okay. This is NOT a very loving thing to do to ourselves. Life in the physical world is one of constant change it seems. There is loss and there are times when it can seem like everything is falling apart, that WE are falling apart. But it is not REALLY so. As Terry Cole-Whittaker used to tell us, *"falling apart is falling together."* We just can't see it yet. We have to trust ourselves and not give in to self-doubt or practically killing ourselves trying to hold everything together.

The main thing is to not give up on ourselves - to stay on our own team. Other people may abandon us, not accept us, hurl all kinds of disapproval on us – there's nothing we can do about that. Defending ourselves just keeps the whole mess activated so it's best to stay in our own yard, turn within and activate our own approval and acceptance. There is no one just like you. No one who has your unique abilities, energy and attributes. If you fall down, it's okay. If you mess up, it's okay you can apologize and clean it up. If you lose some people, it's okay, more are on the way. If you got fired or dumped, it's okay, it's time for something more magnificent. If you were diagnosed with an illness, it's okay, healing is eminent. It's okay, it's okay, it's okay.

Day 5 - THERE IS NOTHING WRONG WITH YOU

Most people have issues and are pretty weird, once you get to know us - so what? Too many people allow excuses to stop them from feeling good about themselves and about their life. Perfection and normalcy are myths used to sell us products and to keep us under control. Freedom and self-love come when we let our freak flag fly high and proud.

I once saw a late night talk show with four very famous and successful people as guests. At a certain point they had what was basically a "weird-off" contest to see which of them had the most phobias and disorders - it ran the gamut from severe OCD, to bi-polar disorder, panic attacks, cutting, and on and on. None of them were what the culture considers "traditionally" attractive. And yet, they were all in happy relationships, owned their own homes and businesses, were very funny, had loving families and friends, were very creative, and seemed to have made peace with themselves.

One of them was Lena Dunham, who almost regularly appears on her HBO show "Girls" naked or nearly naked - and by American TV standards she is considered overweight, though her body is really like most bodies in this country - just the average. She writes the show, so she is CHOOSING to expose herself to a TREMENDOUS amount of hatred, vitriol and attack on social media. But she said it only rarely bothers her and that mostly she doesn't read it. She has not let popular opinion or the culture stop her from living her life as SHE chooses and from what I could tell, no one on the panel that night was taking a poll to see if it was okay for them to be as odd and outrageous as they are. Because odd is what we all are - the cultural standards are insane and cruel.

It's actually staggering to me to realize how many people I knew in the past five years who died either by suicide or by an "accidental" drug overdose - and the drug overdoses were not by regular drug users but by those for whom it was rare to be doing drugs. They were simply trying to ease their mental suffering by unloving means. And in so many cases it was someone who was a health advocate, on magazine covers, under 10% body fat, trying desperately and endlessly to fit the picture of ultra "normalcy" and having it all together and doing it right. They had "washboard abs." They bought into the cultural hypnotism - thinking that self-love and acceptance would come when they finally had it all together and looked perfect and had the perfect home and car and career goals met.

Those people on that TV talk show were the exact opposite. They'd all become successful by saying, *"Fuck the norm. I'm never gonna be that and why would I want to be? I'm going to love myself even with all my flaws and phobias. I'm not waiting for perfection. I'm expressing myself in my art now and am even emphasizing my weirdness instead of hiding it in shame. I'm going to let myself-love and fail and succeed and fall down and prevail even while the haters tweet themselves into hysteria! I'm not waiting, I'm not stopping, and I'm not hiding. The right people will find me if I am vibrating and owning my full self just as I am, and just as I am not."*

People often have a hard time when I say, *"There is nothing wrong with you"* because we live in a society full of armchair psychologists and diagnosticians who are quick to point out just how fucked up we are. But I'm not telling people that they don't have issues and aren't full of weirdness or personality quirks, as most of us are. It's the word WRONG that is key. There may be a lot about you that is weird, that is strange, that is even off-putting - but it is not WRONG. It just is. And that doesn't mean you shouldn't have therapy or take medication if you need or want to - it just means that you've accepted that comparing yourself to anyone else is NOT part of self-love boot camp and will only make you more miserable and depressed. Whatever crazy shit is going on with you, it can be integrated - whether you "fucked up" your body and health somehow or were born with a "different" body or way of thinking and seeing and moving through the world - it can all be used by Life to express more life. You are not broken or alone - there are many lids for even the strangest pots. Strange can be fabulous if you own it.

DAY 6 – WHATEVER YOU SET YOUR MIND TO

You can do whatever you set your mind to do. Most anything that does not affect the free will of another person is possible for YOU to accomplish if you really want it enough and are willing to go for it fully. Breathe that in and see if you actually BELIEVE it or if you just *want* to believe it. But even if you only want to believe it, that is more than enough to get you going in the right direction if you will continue to FEED that desire by imagining, visioning, dreaming and starting to take small action steps in the direction you want to go.

I'm the boot camp Sargent here, which means that I am here to push you to DO even when you don't FEEL LIKE IT. No boot camp Sargent says, *"Drop and give me 50 push ups if you feel like it!"* Remember, this is 90 days of showing up for yourself as a radical act of self-love - NO MATTER WHAT. That may mean FORCING yourself to take a walk on the beach if that is one of the things that you set for yourself to do - even though there is so much work to do and you've been taught to always put yourself dead last. Boot camp is about getting out of that musty old comfort zone and pushing yourself in ways that challenge us when it's so much easier to settle for "same old, same old" without admitting that we've actually given up on our dreams, given up on ourselves. Not on my watch - sorry. That's why boot camps typically end with far fewer participants than were there at the start. The vast majority of people prefer wishing and hoping to actually doing.

It all starts with a desire and imagination, then investigation and willingness, and ultimately the most important step of all - taking some actual physical action. No one is going to give to us what we are unwilling to give to ourselves. No one is coming along to change our lives for the better. The helping hand is at the end of our own sleeve. And once we get in the practice of showing up for ourselves, others will show up for us too. That's how the Universe operates - it reflects back. And once we begin to take some new actions, it begins to build new pathways in the brain and after a while we get a groove going and new ENERGY is released to and through us.

What will you DO to love yourself today?

DAY 7 – REFLECTION AND VISIONING

Congratulations! You've already completed your first week of boot camp and that means ACKNOWLEDGING and celebrating yourself for showing up! It's the perfect time to reflect on how it went and vision the new week ahead of us.

And since self-love is not about perfection, don't look back to find ANYTHING to feel bad or guilty about - nothing to activate feelings of failure and so on. We are looking back to find ONLY where you showed up for yourself in whatever ways you said you would, and even in unexpected ways. We are also looking for any positive shifts in your energy or in the good that came through. Remember, the more we love ourselves, the more GOOD we allow into our lives. So, you may have found that people were kinder to you, or that a new door opened for you, or unexpected gifts came to you, or that you felt better physically or mentally or that your heart was more open. Reflect on these things and give YOURSELF credit - it's not random! Write it down in your journal or in a log if you like.

The next step is to begin to vision for the new week ahead. It's YOUR boot camp, so you can change any part of it that you want or need to once you've reflected on how it's going so far. You can drop what you want and/or add other things. Recently I became aware of ways that I talk myself out of participating in certain aspects of life because of lies I believed about aging. One of my inspirations is Dame Judi Dench. She is 80 years old and still kicking ass! I had always thought that maybe I would mellow with age, but actually I seem to be getting louder and more outrageous - so I've embraced it and agree with Judi saying, *"The older you get the louder you should sing."* She was my favorite part of the recent James Bond movies, playing the part of M. She does not appear to be withdrawing from life at all, so she is part of my inner team of cheerleaders now kicking my butt into gear and off the sofa to DO things that I love to do even if others may judge me. Who are some of your inner mentors that inspire you to GO FOR IT in life?

Boot camp is about paradigm shifting. We begin to think and experience ourselves differently - we are telling different stories about ourselves, life, what we deserve, and what we believe is possible for us. And even if you totally forgot about doing anything you wanted to or said you would in boot camp, let that the fuck go and get back on the highlighted route toward your happy intentions. Failure is not possible here. Start setting the Cosmic GPS now by DECIDING what kind of week you want to have, how you want to feel, what you want to focus on, the energy that you want to activate and bring into the new week. And give yourself a big pat on the back you bold fabulous motherfucker! You are rocking my world with your willingness to keep on keeping on!

DAY 8 – MANIFESTATION MONDAYS (OR ANY DAY)

Never have I ever been as inspired by a group as I am by those who are now participating in the classes I teach, my readers and those who did the online blog of this boot camp! I now consider myself a Consciousness Coach more than anything else when it comes to my work in the world. Since we are not broken, and don't need "fixing" - my job is simply to help keep us in alignment with Source and on our own individual highlighted route.

This is the beginning of a brand new week - week #2, which means that we've already got momentum going in our favor. You are already getting stronger in your own Consciousness through the self loving ACTIONS that you've been taking in your thinking and self-perception - now the deal is to stay the course and keep correcting as we go. Remember, every time you SHOW UP for yourself in some way, it increases the belief and recognition that YOU ARE WORTH THE EFFORT. There is no "should" in this whatsoever - that is self-attack and self-hatred. There is the growing DESIRE to treat yourself as a valuable child of the Cosmos!

Nothing is impossible for you unless YOU say so. HOW is not for you to figure out right now. Program the Cosmic GPS each day and TUNE IN through your intuition and guidance, ASSUMING and EXPECTING that only GOOD lies before you today! The right doors are going to open, the parking places will appear, there will be smiles greeting you and love to light your way if YOU clean up your attitude and ALIGN with it. I've taken to calling the Universe "Charlie

Universe" like the voice from the TV show Charlie's Angels. Charlie is a collective Consciousness that is guiding and directing in a very loving way - no judgment, no withholding, no mental instability - and not a "person" but rather ALL of Infinite Consciousness directing to do today's tasks and providing ALL that is needed to do them with lots of support and encouragement - not to mention perks and bonuses. Life is good. I start my days now with some version of "Good Morning Charlie" and I hear back, "Good morning Angel!" THAT is how Life loves us. You are one of the Universal Angels with a message of radical self-love and acceptance – a message that is fun to deliver and that is sorely needed.

DAY 9 – YOU COULD

At the very least, take the rest of this boot camp as a vacation from the word "should" - don't "should" on yourself during this process. In fact, by the end of this process you will probably find that you've decided to give up that word once and for all. Constantly telling yourself what you should and shouldn't be doing is just another way to heap guilt on yourself - basically, that's not a very loving way to treat the self.

You can simply replace should with the word "could" - and then, you get to make a clearer CHOICE from that place instead of getting caught up in an old story. It's not *"I should do such and such"* but rather, *"I could do such and such."* THEN, decide from that place of freedom rather than guilt, shame or blame.

By this time in boot camp you may have lots of feelings getting stirred up at times and though many of them may feel good, some may not - but it's all good. It means it's working! It doesn't have to be a big deal at all if we relax and trust the process. All this means is being even <u>gentler</u> with yourself - not resorting to bullying yourself or going into overwhelm. So whether it's sadness, or anger, or just general resistance, understand that it's giving you a message of some thoughts or energy that is arising and pay gentle attention to it. Don't STRUGGLE harder to understand it - trust the process and know that you have Guidance you can consult and release it to.

Simply relax and breathe your way through. You can always stop at any moment and take a little time to close your eyes, go inside, soothe yourself and let go. Feelings are just feelings. They are like the weather - they seem to pass more quickly if we don't resist them or get all caught up in them. Listen to what your inner being is telling you and continue to adapt and learn and grow. We're not in a hurry here. We have plenty of time - boot camp has barely started, AND we have the rest of our lives to practice what we learn in this process.

The kind of pushing we want to do here is more like a yoga asana pushing GENTLY into a stretch. We want to have it be just challenging enough to feeeeel the stretch as we breathe into it, but <u>never</u> enough to feel pain or to do ourselves harm. Remember, we're not FORCING self-love. The love is already there, we are simply uncovering it by PRACTICING loving actions which begin to dissolve away the blocks to the awareness of the love that is already there. <u>We are not TRYING to love ourselves, we already DO</u>. It's merely been covered over by habit patterns in thinking and behaving.

DAY 10 – CHEMICALIZATION & THE TURN-AROUND POINT

Now that we are in double-digit days, as Sargent I need to make sure we're not getting sloppy and lazy about form because this is around the time when resistance rears its beautiful head for some folks, myself included. Yes, I'd love to go running back to the cave of my comfort zone and drink 3 glasses of wine and eat half a chocolate cake, follow that up with some chips and a big bowl of pasta in my stretchy pants. By the time I'd wake up it would be Christmas. This is a normal reaction to making positive changes for most of us.

This is what we call "the turn-around point" - it's the place where it gets too uncomfortable and we always quit. We get to a certain point every time and then create some excuse, illness, catastrophe, or whatever, in order to justify giving up on ourselves again and going home. For some it comes this early in the process, for some it comes much closer to the finish line. (And for others, nothing will come up at all and it's an opportunity to move to a new level in an atmosphere of positive encouragement.) The early metaphysical teachers sometimes called this "chemicalization" as a process of what happens when our NEW Thoughts and beliefs start to hit the core of our old thoughts and beliefs. It's like when Alka-Seltzer hits the water and all that fizzing and activity starts everything to be the exact opposite of the old still waters of complacency. It's what can occur when we hit the part of the old belief system that says we can only allow it to get just so good, and no more because *"who are we to be so happy?"*

Sure, it's right about now in the process when I think about quitting and giving up on myself. The old thoughts say, *"Don't be an asshole. Your ship has sailed - you're not going to find love at this age, you're not going to get into shape or lose any weight, you're not going to pay off your debts or save money, you've gone as far in your work as you're ever going to go. You're better off than most so just go back to your safe quiet life of kinda loving yourself instead of loving and encouraging yourself with joyous wild abandon. It's much easier and less painful to resign and call it peace."*

But, that is WHY we have boot camp. Boot camp is about pressing on TOGETHER in this Army of Light. We press on past the lies of the old mental programming. There is NO enemy there to fight. It's just a congregation of thoughts being stirred up before they dissolve - and thoughts can be changed, with patience and consistency. It's training the puppy after the puppy has pooped everywhere and chewed up the rug one too many times for our liking - when we realize *"Oh, this is kind of hard and I'm not in the mood."* We don't give up on the puppy and say, *"Oh fuck it, do whatever you want. Destroy the whole fucking house. I'll just up my medication!"* No, we may not FEEL love for the puppy at that moment, but we do not give up on it, we continue to clean up the mess and TRAIN and TEACH over and over and over again. Slowly we begin to see progress as our puppy begins to grow into a real friend. Remember, this puppy mind will grow to be your most loyal and loving friend over time.

Yes, it can be HARD even to FORCE yourself to book a massage, or take a slow leisurely walk once a day, or to give yourself time to read a book you are enjoying. It can be HARD to SHOW YOURSELF loving ACTIONS on a consistent basis even when it is something sweet like more time to relax, just as hard as eating more healthy or deciding to clean out a hoarded mess because you deserve to live in a clean environment - to BELIEVE that you are worthy of and deserve consistent effort. But ya are Blanche, ya are. NOW, I've written all this for a SPECIFIC PURPOSE, which is to let you know that I know - I understand the challenges are very real. I get it. But this is not permission to start talking about how hard it is for you and all the challenges and so on because in an attraction-based Universe, what do you think happens when you start activating the vibration of *"this is hard for me"* and start putting it out there? That's right, it gets a hell of a lot harder. We are not turning this into a "support group" of sharing our struggles. We assume it's challenging, it's boot camp. And tomorrow, I'll have some ways to turn that around.

I'm staying the course and I'm gonna be here with you every day, rain or shine, because I know the fruits that come from this kind of sowing. Please, keep a log of ANY and all progress you are making and any of the positive shifts in your world. Stick with me here - you are strong and beautiful and Life loves you!!

Day 11 – I Am in the Process Of . . .

This is not the kind of boot camp where the Sargent is screaming in your face to get it right or to pick up the pace. It is the extreme opposite of that. In the same way that when a baby is learning to walk and falls down we don't scream, *"Get up you stupid moron!!"* we are not trying to FORCE ourselves into anything. We are boldly undoing old thought patterns gently and consistently, because this about a daily journey of creating NEW mental habit patterns through our actions.

This means it's not about some end result we're arriving at. By the end of the 90 days we will have established a new way of thinking, but we're not done then. It's an ongoing process of discovery all along the way - it is a process, not an end point that we're going for in this team effort.

Therefore, one of my favorite affirmations to use when I am establishing new thought patterns is *"I am in the PROCESS of* _____.*"* All we do is fill in the blank. I've found that this can be much more helpful than doing an affirmation that is too far from where we currently are in Consciousness that feels like a lie. It's a bridging affirmation from where we <u>are</u> instead of trying to quantum leap to a place we are not ready for. For example, if a home is filled with "stuff" that someone has been hoarding for years and that person wants to create a more loving supportive environment, it won't do him much good to affirm, *"My home is clean, orderly and supportive to my greater good"* when he looks around and sees floor to ceiling clutter. We need bridging affirmations like this one to get us from the old to the new:

- *I am in the process of clearing out the clutter.*
- *I am in the process of being kinder to myself.*
- *I am in the process of taking charge of my health.*
- *I am in the process of believing in myself.*
- *I am in the process of reclaiming my dreams.*
- *I am in the process of creating a more joyful life.*
- *I am in the process of getting more out of life.*
- *I am in the process of bringing sexy back.*
- *I am in the process of releasing old grievances.*
- *I am in the process of creating my dream career.*
- *I am in the process of forgiving.*
- *I am in the process of learning to support myself.*
- *I am in the process of letting go.*
- *I am in the process of increasing my faith and joy.*
- *I am in the process of trusting myself more.*
- *I am in the process of eating healthier and making supportive food choices.*
- *I am in the process of setting healthy boundaries.*

And on and on. What are you in the process of? Probably many things. Try this bridging affirmation as we go through boot camp - particularly if you fall down and need some help in getting back up and feeling good again. A bridging belief helps us get back on the highlighted route more quickly without guilt, blame and shame.

Day 12 – Always Do YOUR Best

Author Anne Lamott mentors many writers and one piece of advice she gives changed my life for the better. She tells them to *"write a shitty first draft"* - because people who are trying to write a perfect first draft never write a book. You write a shitty first draft and then keep on editing and rewriting and shaping and molding it over and over again . . . and still it will never be PERFECT. Perfection is a myth that stops many people from accomplishing their goals because they are afraid they'll be criticized and judged. But you'll be criticized and judged no matter what you do – so let that go kiddo.

I used to dust my home about every 6 weeks because I had to do it "right" - which meant using polish and taking everything off the shelves and so on. So my place was pretty dusty - orderly and neat, but dusty. Then after Anne Lamott gave me permission to do a shitty job, I got a Swiffer and have dusted every week since. This is not PERFECT dusting, but it gets done weekly and it keeps my place clean on an ongoing basis. I've found for myself that most of the time it's better to go to the gym and do a shitty workout, or to take a slower walk around the neighborhood (instead of going on a run) than to do nothing at all. But many of us were taught that if you can't do something "right" don't do it at all – what rubbish. It's showing up that moves us forward.

In the book "The Four Agreements" Don Miguel Ruiz writes to *"always do your best"* but says that our best will change all the time. Our best is different when we are sick than when we are well, for instance. This is very much like yoga class - you may have been more limber two days ago than you are now. So what? It's about SHOWING UP with whatever is YOUR best today - not what others think is your best. I always show up to teach and do my very best every single time, but my best is subject to many variables. And what I think was a fucking fantastic class may not be what Jane Doe thought was a very good class. But even if she hated it, I cannot control what others think or say - I am only in charge of MY best that day. Self-love means that I do not withdraw my love and approval of myself based on the opinions of others.

This is not about copping out or making excuses. Boot Camp requires that we be honest with ourselves about where we are each day, each moment, neither making excuses nor bullying ourselves. Making a mistake, or falling down is not a reason to quit, give up on yourself or go back to square one. Maybe you fell down and started criticizing yourself again, or feeling shame and guilt about who you are, or have been judging some aspect of your life. Fine. Let it go, get up, and keep moving forward. We just keep getting back on the highlighted route over and over again, even if we got lost and ended up back where we started. We're all in this together and it IS already working. I love the movie Private Benjamin for so many reasons, but one of them is that she DID keep finding her strength and determination, even though it went against all her programming. She'd been programmed to believe she couldn't take care of herself, wasn't strong, couldn't do anything, needed a man to take care of her. And even after she'd make good progress, she'd sell herself out again . . . for a little while. But once this process has begun, it's very hard to STAY under the spell. Keep going. You're doing great. She woke up and you are waking up too!

Day 13 – Releasing the Naysayers

If we are going to activate our self-love, then we are not only going to need to let go of old negative thought patterns and habits, but we need to have healthy boundaries in our relationships. When I first began this journey to self-love back in the 1980's, the first thing I had to do was leave an organization I was involved in which was very abusive. In fact, there were several relationships in which I had to set some boundaries about what kind of treatment I would accept. In fact, my very first affirmation ever was: *"There is no yelling at Jacob."*

"Spiritual" types often have a problem with this and will "spiritualize" accepting all kinds of unloving words and behavior from others under the guise of "acceptance" and "forgiveness." These are gross misunderstandings of acceptance and forgiveness. No one gets to call you names, criticize or attack you no matter how "well meaning" they are or how many times they end it with, *"because I love you"* - unless you still believe you deserve to be treated that way, which means that being in this boot camp is just what the metaphysician ordered. You do NOT deserve to be anything but loved and respected.

Hopefully this entry today will not pertain to any of you - but it's very necessary for me to put out there if even one of you are tolerating relationships that are demeaning or draining your of your confidence, peace, joy or Light. If you are surrounding yourself with people who don't support you, don't believe in you, and aren't bringing anything good to the table . . . then RELEASE may be exactly what is up for you now.

Now, that doesn't necessarily mean you have to confront everyone directly. Remember, everything reflects our Consciousness so when we TRULY change the inner, the outer will eventually reflect this. When we begin to set healthy boundaries AND practice release, people either step up to the plate and change their behavior, or they vibrate out of your space because they are no longer a vibrational match to your self-love.

Affirmation: *I now release and am released from everything and everybody that is no longer a part of the Divine Plan of my life. I now expand quickly into the Divine Plan for my greater peace, joy, love and abundant good! I am a magnet for loving supportive people and my world is filled with encouragement and love!*

Day 14 – Reflect and Review

Boot Campers, you made it through the first two weeks! Congratulations on a job well done. How are you feeling? I hope you are feeling very proud of yourself for having made it because that's what it's about. It's not about what you "accomplished" or what you did or didn't do. It's about the inner dialogue that you are having with yourself about <u>everything</u> in your world and how much more is coming from your kinder more supportive attitude than from any old negative programming.

I taught a class in Santa Barbara yesterday - and had a ball and taught the shit out of that class. But that doesn't mean I did not still have those old bullying thoughts of: *"Jacob that was terrible. You are an idiot. You said all the wrong things and barely any of the right ones. You need to go get a job a the mall and stop all this foolishness."* But I know that's just an old echo from the past and that in self-love boot camp we neutralize that voice with opposing information - so I thought about the faces of those who seemed to be having a great time in class instead. I thought about those who had tears in their eyes at times when I was encouraging the class. I don't even bother addressing the old negative programming. I just keep deleting it by running the NEW encouraging programs.

What I would like to suggest to you at this point, is beginning an ongoing list titled: "My Positive Aspects." The purpose of this list is to continue making the shift away from the invisible list of "where I fucked up, the things that are wrong with me" and replace it with the very VISIBLE LIST of "where I am doing great or improving, and what is wonderful about me." Remember, words are containers for POWER. Perhaps there is nothing it all the multiverse as powerful as words. *"In the beginning was the word."* And with the word everything is made or destroyed. We are in a process of burning and building. We are burning off the old negative programming and building UP the new programming of love and confidence and self esteem - and ultimately, it will all come down to WORDS. The words that we FEED and FOCUS ON in our self-talk is what will grow and begin to completely take over. It's how we learn best - through words that are backed up with actions.

It's why grade school walls are so often covered with BIG BIG WORDS. And I am suggesting that you might want to start to go from small affirmations around the house to BIG WORDS ON YOUR WALLS AND BULLETIN BOARDS AND FRIDGE. Just single or double words that will begin to seep into your programming, whether they are about yourself, or what you want to manifest in your life, something you want to be or do or have or experience. Words like: success, parent, wealthy, vibrant health, vacation home, loved, appreciated, husband, money, great ideas, gifted, prolific, amazing, valuable, worthy, talented, wise, loving, caring, centered, and on and on. What single word best represents some of the things you want to activate and amplify in your Consciousness on a daily basis?

Words are what got me on this road to begin with. Where I grew up, there was no one encouraging me, no one telling me I could do . . . anything. My town was about athletics and nothing else and since I was not that, I was nothing. So, I had to do it myself. My walls were covered with BIG PICTURES AND WORDS WORDS WORDS. I would buy those inspiring posters with slogans on them and I actually had a "Don't Quit" poster on my dorm room wall when I first sent myself away to college. I cannot count the times that I would read it when I was trembling with fear that I was in fact NOT going to make it at all - that I was running out of money, that I was in way over my head, that I was failing some classes, and that I was too stupid to learn anything. I would read those WORDS and DECIDE to keep going. And by doing that, at the exact right moment, and sometimes at the 11th hour, the exact right door would open to take me in a new direction. Words. A very very big deal.

DAY 15 – THE LIFE YOU DESERVE

So what is this Army of Light I sometimes mention really about? Simple, shining Light into a world that is fascinated and hypnotized by darkness. But you cannot shine the Light as fully and BRIGHTLY as possible if you are blocking it with feelings of unworthiness yourself. And there is no reason whatsoever for you to feel unworthy in the least. You are such a special child of Light with so much to give. And if you think I am just blowing smoke up your ass, cool. You need to have a lot of smoke blown up your ass because it has not happened to you nearly enough. Perhaps you don't know that the physician's of old used to LITERALLY insert a pipe up the asses of people and then blew smoke up there in order to resuscitate a heart that had stopped beating!

Well, I am here blowing smoke up YOUR ass to try to resuscitate your dying or dead ego. That may sound shocking to you because the "spiritual/religious" nuts have told you that the ego is a bad thing. It's yet another fabulous creation of the Universe that's been demonized in order to control you. But YOU are awake now and cannot be fooled so easily into hating parts of yourself. The ego is a fabulous divine thing. Freud said that the ego is the part of consciousness that experiences itself as an individual being. It's not ALL that you are, but without it you are merely a drone of the Universe knocking into walls and having no awareness of where you end and another person begins. You need a STRONG HEALTHY EGO in order to DO what you need to do every day and in order to FEEL good about yourself. Yes, you are one with all Life and the Universe, but as an individualized expression of that one Life, that one Mind. Your desires, and quirks, and preferences, and differences, and all that you experience as "I" is very important to the Universal expansion of Life itself. The ego is as divine as any other creation of the God-Source and if it is not demonized, it will be yet another great ally to help you become all you were created to be. It will help you to keep going when you've been rejected or failed a few dozen or hundred times. It is not the enemy; it is another aspect of GOD Itself. It can take you by the hand and give you that extra PUSH you need to finish the race, to ask for the raise, to stop the abuse, to start the new business, to go to the party, to shine in the audition, to finish writing the song, to adopt the baby, to CREATE THE LIFE YOU WANT AND DESERVE. It will help you BELIEVE IN YOURSELF when perhaps everyone around you does not.

So, BE YOU - fabulous amazing, crazy, normal, mundane, exotic, too loud, too quiet, unique fucking amazing you. The UNIVERSE loves YOU being YOU. I know how many of your accomplishments have gone unnoticed. I know that you have worked very hard and overcome many obstacles and challenges. I know how hard you try and I also know that you have been ridiculously and needlessly hard on yourself at time. And I also know that this has at times frustrated you and made you hard on others, at least in your mind. That is all drawing to an end now soldier because we are integrating ALL the wonderful parts of yourself into a whole, sane, brilliant being - not different than you are, not a "better" self, but one that is whole - a team that is all going in the same joyful direction instead of at war with itself. When your ego becomes accepted, balanced and healthy, what you find is that the ego can actually go out to do more good in the world WITHOUT coming from a place of self-sacrifice.

Beware of people who teach you to hate or fear your ego because they have the most dangerous egos of all. You NEED a healthy ego in order to ENJOY your life. And a healthy ego is what helps to push you past your self-imposed illusory limitations.

This is the start of a great week of strengthening your realizations that you DESERVE to have all your dreams come true, to have your efforts succeed, to have your accomplishments honored by YOU even if no one else notices, and that the days of being hard on yourself are coming to an end. Pushing yourself forward out of determination and a desire for something is admirable. Pushing yourself out of loathing, self-hatred and fear is just that "cold war" religious programming trying to play itself out again. In just a few weeks, you are already going past that place. You've grown stronger and more determined than you know. You are one of my heroes!

Day 16 – Remember Who You Are

You may spend the major part of your days sitting in a cubicle, or chasing around little children, or taking out kitty litter and watching TV, or any number of mundane tasks. But what you do is not who you are. Do not confuse your "who" with your "do" because they can be very different. And as an expansive creative extension of Source Energy, you may be many things in many different ways.

Neville Goddard says, "Man is all Imagination" and it's true that we live far more in our imagination, in our mind, than anywhere else. It can be terrible or it can be wonderful depending on what we are imagining. Many of you who've been with me a while know that I have many different "Who's" that I experience myself as at any given period of time. I may see myself as the Boot Camp Sargent of the Dream Academy Starship while I am balancing the bank account. I may see myself as a Wizard Professor of Esoteric Mysticism while duplicating CD's in my tiny laundry closet. I may see myself as Secret Agent Angel 007 on a mission to bring Light to the coffee shop. Or I may see myself as the last of the red-hot lovers. I surround myself with things that remind me WHO I am while in the midst of the ordinary day. It's so easy and helpful to do. You may have a tiny figurine of a ballet dancer next to your computer mouse pad, or a photo of that trip to Brazil from 10 years ago, or a bathroom tile from your dream home, or . . . .whatever reminds you of who you are inside.

It begins in mind, in Imagination, and it is this that feeds our hearts and activates that pure love of a child for living and expressing. The whole Universal Chorus is singing to us more loudly all the time, *"Remember who you are. Remember. Remember. It's safe to remember who you are. REMEMBER. Wake up to who you are. Pay attention. It's in you. Wake up. Remember who you are."*

I know it's already been happening in you. You're starting to remember. It may bring up some emotions. That's okay. Relax and breathe. Give yourself permission to remember the beautiful brilliant Creator that you are inside. Remember who you are. AS you remember, you are summoning Source Energy through you - the Energy that creates worlds. This Imaginative faculty is what opens new doors for you and quickens your vibration to the place where what has been imagined is drawn into physical manifestation. How fabulous is that?

DAY 17 – SHUT THAT PARTY DOWN

"Without launching into mountainous waves of self-pity, how are you?" is one of my favorite lines from the holiday movie, The Man Who Came to Dinner. Of course that was impossible because the character this was addressed to managed to feel put-upon while in the lap of luxury. That's what makes it a comedy, but that is also what makes many real lives a depressing tragedy. There's an enormous amount of healthy employed upper and middle class income people having pity parties in very nice homes in good neighborhoods, feeling sorry for themselves in a way that beggars in India do not.

And as someone who used to keep a permanent party set up in the corner exclusively used for pity parties, I have come to believe they are the most corrosive and violent kind of self-abuse and are almost a type of insanity. It is a way of myopically focusing on the worst while negating and dismissing all the good in one's life. It's shocking how often it is done in absolute isolation in a nice place when right outside the door there are people to play with and things to do. Instead of joining someone for dinner or gathering together to watch that TV show, old and new hurts are nursed and gone over and over again mentally off in a corner somewhere. The 100 good Yelp reviews are ignored in order to keep reading the 2 negative ones and committing them to memory. Even the dog only loves you because you feed her! THAT is how ridiculous and dangerous this "party" can become when we allow our mind to twist everything into more evidence that we are not loved or appreciated and that life is just too hard for someone as sensitive, artistic, heart-centered and as misunderstood as we are. It's just not fair!

One of the most famous Bible stories is of the prodigal son who asks for his inheritance from his father early, then goes off, spends it all on loose living and returns home as a beggar asking to just work for his father as a servant. The father runs out to meet him with jewelry and gives him a big party to celebrate his return home. But the OTHER son is pissed off. Where is his party? Where is his jewelry and celebration for having STAYED and done the right thing all along? Why doesn't anyone notice him and recognize how hard he's worked at always doing the right thing? Well, I suspect that he might have been a self-righteous drag, but I'm just guessing here. The other brother was the fuck-up but at least he did know how to have a good time. He wasn't exactly happy and self-loving either obviously but at least he was off the couch not marinating in victim thinking. And the father's answer to the son who stayed home was, *"Son, you LIVE here 24/7 and have everything you need to have a party every day. Why are you waiting around for someone else to do it for you when everything I have is already yours?"* When I GOT this, it changed my whole fucking life!!

The whole Universe is available to us if we will look UP from our pitiful table for one and get up and OUT into the world! ALL the sunshine and fresh air is available to us right outside that door. WE are free to give ourselves any kind of party we want - it can be a pity party or a celebration of another day of LIVING LIFE! The theme is up to us. About 10 years ago when I woke up to this, I began TREATING MYSELF the way I kept waiting for others to treat me. I got into the DAILY HABIT of writing down what had gone RIGHT in my life in the past 24 hours, instead of focusing on what went wrong. I wrote down where I had gotten it

RIGHT instead of ruminating on where I had fucked up and let myself down and been a Charlie Brown. I started to take myself out to lunch as my own little celebratory party and I stopped inviting people who were a drag or who wanted to bend my ear for an hour about their problems. I had to remove the *"yes, but . . . "* from my life - the ways in which I would LOOK at the good but then INVALIDATE it somehow. *"Yes, I live in this great home, but I don't OWN it! Yes, my bills are paid, but I don't have any retirement saved! Yes, my body is healthy but it's getting old and out of shape!"* and on and on. These are all ways of CHOOSING NOT TO BE HAPPY. Even if you have suffered MAJOR losses and devastating circumstances, all that means is that you need help and that it will take some time to go through the healing process, but marinating in self-pity and *"why me?"* is NOT helpful or healing.

So, one of the ways I see my role as Boot Camp Sargent in your life is as a kind of Mary Poppins here to be sure that you are getting up and out of any tendency to isolate in feelings of self-pity. It's still something I have to watch out for in myself, which is why I am so diligent about doing my daily pages of writing down just how great life is. And of course, once I began treating myself well, it began to be reflected in my outer world - because THAT is how Consciousness operates. First the emotional inner journey, and then the outer manifestations will follow, spit spot! You may also accelerate your own journey if you go help someone else and take the focus off of your own worries. Distraction from yourself can often be just what the metaphysician ordered.

Day 18 – Love Can Be Boring

One of the problems with real love is that it can just be so damn boring. We talk about love being an ACTION - and mostly the actions are mundane, boring and frequently thankless. The problem here is that when most people say "love" what they really are thinking of is some form of ROMANCE. I'm not even talking about sexual love here but the romantic idea of that soul connection to anyone or anything. We have all kinds of romantic fantasies about people, work, success, family life, and on and on and on.

But real love can sometimes be mind-numbingly boring and mundane. Changing endless diapers and cleaning up messes, coaching the kids baseball team and having the parents scream at you, figuring out something nutritious to make for dinner every day for decades on end, keeping on top of the paperwork at work - consistently coming from love is an endless job and has no "awards season" coming down the line.

However, it is a little bit easier to press on with other people and outer situations at least. We have REASONS why. If we want to keep the job we love, we press through the boring or overwhelming parts. If we want the kids or pets to not die we push through and figure out something good to feed them. If we want the relationship to continue, we put time and effort into it. When it comes to other people and situations, we don't usually wait until we're "inspired" or super motivated to actually DO the actions of love and caring. But with self-love, it's a little trickier and takes more tolerance for the boring mundane expressions of self-care.

Many of us give up on ourselves far too quickly and easily. We make excuses for not following through with even the smallest efforts at times because "it feels silly" or stupid to force ourselves to do it when there is often no immediate payoff.

It's another reason why addiction is so prevalent - the addiction gives such an INSTANT FEELING and we are a generation of people who prefer instant gratification. In fact, it would be staggering for all the experts to find out just how much addiction is really the result of nothing more than the result of boredom and impatience. Taking care of ourselves over and over and over again and making good choices would make for a TV show that would be cancelled 3 minutes into the first airing because it's just not sexy or stimulating. Taking the vitamin, meditating, balancing the checking account, keeping the place somewhat clean and orderly so you have a nice environment - basically endlessly showing up for ourselves is not always super romantic or exciting and that is often one of the big underlying reasons we stop at a certain point.

BUT HERE IS THE GOOD NEWS my dear Jedi Soldiers of Light. If we press on through the feeling of "no feeling" long enough, our activity kicks into being A HABIT and not an endless daily choice. This is also why boot camp is 90 days and not a weekend workshop. It gets us through the resistance until the new loving ACTIONS become habitual, like brushing your teeth, or bathing, or having a morning cup of coffee. We're not debating and questioning it anymore, we're just doing it without need to feel inspired or motivated. Self-criticism is nothing more than a mental habit pattern.

Self-love is nothing more than a mental habit pattern. And habits can be changed very unsexily and methodically through repetition of a NEW action. So again, I'm here to tell you that YOU ARE WORTH THE EFFORT. And though the habit itself may not be all that exciting, what you begin to attract into your world as a result of the habit can be very exciting and romantic and inspiring and all kinds of juicy feeling things. Boot camp is about "the law of the farm" - you cannot cram on a farm. You cannot spend the whole sowing and growing season doing nothing, but then at the final day of summer cram in all the planting like we used to cram for an exam in high school. We are working with natural laws of the Universe here - and for long-lasting beneficial change, there is no real substitute for putting in the daily work. Harvest season WILL come and I assure you it is bountiful, abundant and life giving.

Day 19 – Keep Blinders Handy

This is yet another way of "running your own race" and keeping to your own path. It works amazingly well for me and since moving here to the desert of Palm Springs I've seen and felt the soothing restorative wonders of having less and less of an idea what other people are up to regardless of how curious I may be about what's going on in the lives of other people. And the less I know about what other teachers or writers and such are doing, the happier I become in my own work, the more confident I feel, and the more I love and appreciate what I am doing without judging it or myself.

How often we use our blinders will be an extremely individual thing of course. There are those who get really charged up and inspired to new ideas by watching what others are being, doing or having in their lives so they may only need blinders when working on something that demands extreme concentration and/or solitude. I find that the more I wear mine the better off I am because I still manage to see and know plenty of what is going on in the world and around me. But a little bit of that goes a very very very long way with me these days. It's far too easy to get into "compare and despair" and start feeling like something is wrong over here in my own yard. And I wasted quite a bit of time being distracted by people and things that were really not on my path and only took me off my highlighted route. Have you?

I often think how different the lives of people might be without magazines endlessly showing us not only what other people are up to, but giving endless advice on what we should be eating, wearing, drinking, watching, and how we should be exercising, raising our children, and on and on and on. Even if you don't buy them, it seems like there are a thousand of them at every checkout at the grocery or drug stores. I've been making a point to just not even glance at them anymore. For you, it may be something entirely different. It may be making a point not to listen at work to the company gossip if that gives you anxiety and stress. It may be removing yourself from certain social media, or the giving up of some things that are ultimately not relaxing or not stimulating in a positive way - basically "time wasters" that keep you from doing things that would make a more positive difference in your life. I'm not talking about endlessly keeping a nose to the grindstone either, but there are many things offered to us as "relaxation" or "recreation" that end up doing us subtle and cumulative harm. I LOVE to watch TV, but I've drastically reduced my viewing, not because TV is bad for me but because I was watching a lot of stuff I didn't even enjoy so it wasn't even relaxing.

I've been enjoying my life more and more all the time lately as a lot of things are now in my rear view mirror, and my blinders block a lot of other non-essentials out. I see the goals in front of me and am much better able to not get distracted from where I'm going. As you continue on dear boot camper, consider if you might benefit from a nice set of blinders for certain areas or times in your life now to help you stay focused on what matters most to you now. Blinders are how horses keep moving toward their goal instead of being distracted by all the things they see going on around them. Very useful for horses and for people who want to thrive and succeed in life.

Day 20 – Invest Wisely and Consciously

Oh, how it would have saved me so much time, energy and resources if someone had taught me this at 17! It is such a simple and obvious message - *support that which supports you.* GO WHERE THE LOVE IS. WALK THROUGH THE OPEN DOORS. Withdraw support from that which does not support you. It's so obvious that it's silly, and yet so many of us miss this. We love those who do not love us. We give to those who are not grateful. We are there for that which is not there for us. This is one of the hallmarks of a lack of self-love. When we are not loving ourselves, we do not honor our gifts, energy or contributions enough and we can waste them rather than investing them.

Once I learned this (and continue to relearn it at times) my suffering decreased dramatically and the love began to increase exponentially. It took me such a long time to learn this and perhaps that makes me the perfect one to teach it. I could write volumes about all the people I showed up for who disappeared when it was my turn. The authors and teachers I supported and promoted, because I really believed in them and believed we were friends, who turned to vapor when my books came out or I was teaching a class. The friends who I listened to for hours and hours on end in their grief and fear who only called when they had a problem and always seemed to forget to tell me about their party. All the free gifts I gave away at lectures and classes to people who would then honor and praise OTHER teachers and groups who did nothing but take their money and try to sell them more shit. The lunches I bought people, all the furniture I gave away to friends, and the ways that I kept trying to help,

help, help when really it was not appreciated. I was a giver who attracted "takers" who never felt any desire at all to give back - they did their giving elsewhere, to people and places that were not helping them a fraction as much as I was. When I think of the classes and lectures I paid to attend where the teacher only made us feel guilty, not spiritual enough, gave us MORE work to do and chastised us to heal and fix everyone else and to serve serve serve . . . well, I was still under the spell of religion/spirituality and needed to wake up. I cannot tell you how freeing it is to be post-spiritual and not under the tyranny of all the "rules" of modern competitive spirituality in which each person is trying to appear more enlightened than the next where someone is constantly "correcting" you on how to be different than you are.

It's not the fault of any of these people or organizations I was dealing with. I was not there under court order and I could have left at any time. They were just players in the drama of my belief system at the time. It was MY fault for not honoring myself enough to step away and realize that I was the one CHOOSING to be there. No one is doing it to us. These things are a reflection of our own Consciousness and until we are willing to STOP investing in situations that are one-sided, the pattern will never stop and we will have depleted ourselves. In truth, I was trying to EARN people's love and approval through DOING and GIVING and HELPING and SERVING instead of just BEING - and once we are for sale in that way, we are IMMEDIATELY in the bargain bin and we've announced to the Universe that we are not worth much. NO ONE IS DOING IT TO US. It is the result of a lack of love of self and the belief that WE are somehow responsible for others - not believing that we are enough even if we aren't always giving and helping and saving and doing.

And the **great news** is that the very second I turned my thinking around, gifts and love started coming, coming, coming from all different directions. Once I released all those old hostages from what I thought they should be doing, I saw how many other people were there all the time offering love, praise, approval, fun, companionship, opportunities, open doors and so much more!! The Light is always there, even when we've turned to be hypnotized by the shadow instead. Remember, Light moves at the speed of light! It does not take long at all to turn around a negative pattern and to start reaping the harvest of right thinking. But we have to stop blaming others - we have to release the hostages and realize that they were just the reflection of our Consciousness at that time, but now we are in a different mindset and are attracting new and reciprocal relationships. AND I learned to start giving where the giving was appreciated and not just taken for granted so that I felt like I was really investing rather than just casting my pearls to farm animals that have no use for pearls.

Again, we don't live the life we deserve; we live the life we THINK we deserve. The Universe just mirrors back to us our own Consciousness and thinking. It's just a thought, and a thought can be changed.

Day 21 – Where's Your Proof?

Life leaves clues. The way we can prove something is by the evidence we have - otherwise it's just another cockamamie theory. Where there is love, you will find the clues left behind, the evidence.

I probably have fewer people in my life than ever before, and yet the love is at an all-time high! In fact, it even makes me FEEL HIGH at times. And the evidence just keeps mounting. Some folks make a point of being very direct about it - they say, "I love you" directly to me, or they write it in emails and cards. It always feels so wonderful and heart warming to hear or read those words and I do enjoy it greatly. However, let's not forget that there is nothing cheaper in the whole Universe than words.

In spiritual circles it can be one of the most overused and manipulative phrases you hear - cheap talk of love, love, love. But where there is real love, there will be acts of love to back it up. There are people in my life who never say it to me, never write it in a card, and yet I FEEL their love very deeply and profoundly. There are others who say it all the time, and it's just sounds like white noise in the background because I know they will break every promise, take without ever giving, not show up, not follow through with me, not even think of me unless they want or need something from me, not honor my boundaries or show respect for my wishes, will not make time for me, and so on. But they think saying, *"I love you"* will cancel all of that out - and this works for a lot of people simply because so many are starving for love. But do not be fooled by appearances and do not be the kind of person who is forever spouting a love that has no action behind it. We must be DOERS OF THE WORD, and not just hearers and speakers of the word.

By now, as we are completing week 3 of boot camp, I know that many of you are seeing the evidence of self-love starting to reveal itself to you. Saying, "I love you" in the mirror every day is a lovely practice, but where's your evidence? Look for the clues. Are you being kinder to yourself in general? Do you have less guilt and shame? Do you have more inner peace? Are you keeping your word to yourself more? Are you showing up for yourself? Are you tolerating less bullshit and standing up for yourself? Are you allowing yourself to believe in your dreams more? Do you make time for yourself to take care of yourself in ways that matter and are fruitful?

If at the end of a busy workweek your boss said, *"Carol we really really love you here and think very very highly of you, you know that, but we've decided not to pay you this week. In fact, we've decided to only pay you when it's convenient for us, if and when we feel like it. We're also cancelling all your benefits and are taking away your vacation and sick days. However, we just adore you and hope that you will continue to work for us and show up on time every day and keep your end of the bargain - oh, and we'd like to yell at you and blame you for things if that's not too much trouble. Thanks, you're a doll!"* This is the love that has no evidence, no clues, and no proof. It's the spiritual platitude used to both soothe and manipulate. It also makes the person saying it feel better about themselves even while they are being extremely unloving in their actions. Abusive spouses are notorious for saying very loving things after a violent episode in order to ease their guilt and to keep the abused person in the relationship.

You'd be better off going to work for a company that doesn't tell you that you're "family" and is highly impersonal but pays you on time, promotes you when you deserve it, keeps their word about vacations and benefits, and are run by standard business practices rather than on whims and emotions. Because again, LOVE IS NOT A FEELING, it's an action that leaves evidence and clues. The feeling of affection is but one small aspect of love. It's FABULOUS, but it's only a small part of what love really is. And if you're going to say *"I love you"* and you want it to have real depth and oomph, say WHY and WHAT you love specifically. This is VERY powerful with mirror work too. Don't just look in the mirror and say *"I love you"* say what you love about that person in the mirror, the qualities, the talents, the behaviors, the physicality and so on. This makes it go TURBO!

So, if you haven't already, start looking for the clues that your self-love is growing and you will begin to notice that the ACTIONS are stimulating and CREATING the FEELING. The more we take these LOVING ACTIONS toward ourselves, the more our FEELINGS of confidence, self approval, self respect and genuine affection will grow and grow and grow.

Day 22 – Be A Gracious Receiver

Boot Campers! We're starting week 4 already! Look how far you've come. You are doing it. You're still here and you ARE making progress. I'm proud of you and of us. Let's keep right on going. This shit is working and getting more exciting as we go . . .

Another big aspect of self-love is the ability to accept and graciously receive good when it comes. Something that has always helped me tremendously is taking advantage of opportunities, but not of people. Every step of the way I've had tremendous help from other people to not only reach my goals, but also sometimes just to survive and get by. Over and over again the doors have opened for me at just the right times and false pride would only have kept me from walking through them to my greater good. Sometimes people mistake pride for confidence and self-love, but it's really just another form of resistance. We all need help. No one is dependent or independent - we are all interdependent. Believing we can do it all ourselves is not self-love and confidence, it's misguided commitment to struggle.

Yes, a lot of people have opened doors for me, taken me in, done me enormous favors, and I've succeeded only because I accepted their lift up - but I also never took advantage of their kindness. And because I then stepped up to the plate and made sure that they felt good about helping me, I grew into a greater sense of myself as capable. I didn't just sit back and take advantage of their help and let them do everything for me. I let them teach me what I didn't know and I not only became better, I learned how to help others in the same way.

We all need help, so make it EASY to help you. ASK, and then be a gracious receiver and do YOUR part. Don't ask someone to drive you to the airport and then not have started packing yet when they arrive at your house. ASKING for exactly what you want takes confidence and self-love - hinting, whining, wishing, beating around the bush - these come from fear and are NOT who you are anymore, remember? Ask for what you want and then PREPARE to receive it.

The thinking of the world is backwards and upside down. In fact, I call the wonderful reality I live in, "Opposite World" in which everything is the opposite of what the culture has taught us. We tend to think that if we had more confidence, we would ask for the raise or ask that person out on a date. The truth is, asking for a raise or asking the person out on a date is what creates confidence in us. Terry Cole Whittaker used to tell us, *"The thing you're waiting to have happen before you make the commitment, happens AFTER you make the commitment."* Commit to asking for what you want and becoming a gracious receiver of your good boot camper. Life goes to those who step out and CLAIM it for themselves. Courage. Confidence. Boldness. You can do this.

Day 23 – Stop Doubting & Second-Guessing Yourself

It is a radical act of self-love to live your life the way you choose, without apology or explanation. And many spiritual disciplines are rooted in having people constantly doubt, diminish and abase themselves even in sweet subtle ways, *"lean not unto thine own understanding . . . of myself I can do nothing . . . I do not perceive my own best interests"* and so on. It's another way of relinquishing your own power and intellect - and it is not self-love. YOU have INFINITE Intelligence WITHIN you to help you understand through clear thinking and seeing - and what we do not know, we can learn through investigation and a thirst to know and understand - not everything of course, but often more than we would think. YOU are meant to be the authority in your life, not some bible or book or experts or the peanut gallery. This is not blasphemous; it is the Divine within us expressing Itself.

Too many people cripple themselves with the endless insecurity of *"Did I do the right thing, am I doing the right thing, will I do the right thing?"* to the point of paralysis and/or great anxiety. It is nothing more than fear, fear, and more fear. Confidence is not the arrogance of thinking we are never wrong or cannot make a mistake or fail, but it is a boldness to dare to step out and risk once we've carefully considered and investigated possible outcomes. We are not foolish, but we are BRAVE enough to stand behind our own decisions and choices even if we change our minds later on. Wishy-washy is not a true spiritual attribute anyhow. Living according to YOUR OWN AUTHORITY is one of the most spiritual things you could possibly do.

When you start loving yourself in this radical way it may upset the apple carts of those around you. They may not want you to change in this way - you used to be so humble, or compliant, or endlessly patient, or agreeable as you sat quietly in the corner, and now you are so "out there" and unpredictable. You put yourself first instead of dead last and everyone knows how unspiritual and sinful that is!! You are supposed to "die to self" and serve, serve, serve others. i.e.: *"you need to stop selfishly doing what YOU want to do and be selfless and do what I want you to do!"* The ones who suppress themselves the most will be the ones who shout you down the loudest. Why, you even eat the last cookie now instead of asking if anyone else wants it!!

I'm here to encourage you to unleash your own innate greatness even though the spiritual ones may tell you that only God is great and you are just a blip in eternity. Well, you are a God-blip and that means you have a God-given brain and desire and inherent greatness waiting to be birthed every moment as you claim your own unique destiny. It takes courage and boldness. When you make a decision, make that decision right instead of making it wrong. Get behind your own choices instead of giving in to old echoes of past mistakes or failures. Remember, dying of embarrassment is only a phrase, it's not literal. I've embarrassed myself a million times and I'm still here doing great - and actually doing better every day as we move forward in this boot camp. I first learned all of this year's ago in Emerson's essay on "Self-Reliance" but it's time again for me to take it to a deeper level in my daily experience, and it has certainly rocked a lot of boats, but from the emails I am receiving, it's also the most powerful teaching I've done in these 30 years of writing and speaking.

Investigate, study, think things through, get advice, do what you need to in your decision making processes and of course take into consideration loved ones whom your decisions will affect, but ultimately YOU are the only one living your life. This is not a dress rehearsal. Every night is opening night and you are center stage so you may as well play to the balcony so that they know you were here! And as Bette Midler says, *"fuck em if they can't take a joke!"*

"Speak what you think now in hard words and to-morrow speak what to-morrow thinks in hard words again, though it contradict every thing you said to-day. — 'Ah, so you shall be sure to be misunderstood.' — Is it so bad then to be misunderstood? Pythagoras was misunderstood, and Socrates, and Jesus, and Luther, and Copernicus, and Galileo, and Newton, and every pure and wise spirit that ever took flesh.
To be great is to be misunderstood."
- Ralph Waldo Emerson

Day 24 – Relax, Let Go, Surrender

Take a nice deep breath and really let go on the exhale . . . ahhhhhhhh. That's right. Let it all go. Release all struggle and resistance and allow yourself to coast for a while now. You've been going going going - it's time to take advantage of all the momentum you've created and let it carry you without struggle or effort.

It's time to float downstream in the peace of the Great Mother's arms as you let her love hold you afloat in these healing waters. There's nothing to do, nothing to get or fix or change - just a gentle opening to receive. Let all your thoughts slow down and allow your mind to expand into its natural state of spaciousness.

Let the Universe love you today. You cannot earn it and nothing you've ever done, no mistake you've ever made, no matter how badly you think you fucked up, none of that can keep this liquid love from you. Melt into it now as you let go of all your burdens and fears and worries. Let go of your guilt and shame and blame. Release any negative thoughts you have about who and what you are - let them drain out of you into these living waters as you simply relax and breathe, relax and breathe.

Walk in love today and know that the past is over. You are walking into a new day, a new moment, and a new opportunity to experience the peace and love and limitless joy that are your Divine Inheritance. Forgiveness is yours. Release is yours. Peace is yours. Let it in. You're home.

Day 25 – Believe It In

Your destiny is going to be whatever YOU say it is. It's not so much a matter of believing in it but more a matter of ***believing it in***. You BELIEVE it into existence through your imagination first, and then with your aligned thoughts, words and ACTIONS.

It does take effort - everything takes effort. It takes effort for me to sit here typing this to you. But we tend to confuse effort with struggle - and they are very different frequencies. It's not about struggling your dreams and visions into manifestation. Let go of the struggle. Focus more on connecting to your own inner wisdom and then following your intuition and call to joy. A lot of the work may be very boring and methodical at times, but if you are following your vision for yourself, it won't feel like struggle though it will take a lot of consistent effort.

It's important to discipline the mind in order to enjoy the journey even when it's pretty bumpy and hard. It's a shift in attitude. It takes attention and a solid practice of gratitude and appreciation not just for the good in your life, but for YOURSELF and all your efforts. Many of them will go unnoticed, but YOU will know and it will help you to BELIEVE. Usually people will start to take notice long after you've stopped caring if they notice or not. It's not their job to believe in you - it's yours.

To believe what? To believe that happiness is possible for you - not just later on, but right now. To believe that the Universe is a friendly Force that supports you. To believe that the right doors will open for you at the right time. To believe that you deserve to thrive and to have a wonderful life. To believe that you are loved and lovable - and so much more. Don't misunderstand, I'm not saying that you will get everything you want and your life will look the way you thought it would look in form. I'm saying don't give up - because the journey itself, if you discipline yourself to enjoy it and make the best of it, will bring into manifestation all the people, places, resources and circumstances for a great and grand adventure in which you become the woman or man that you were born to be.

Day 26 – Slow Down to the Speed of Love

Too often, people feel bereft of love when they are actually surrounded by it. One of the most powerful ACTIONS of self-love, of love at all, is paying careful deliberate attention. As someone who has been teaching for 30 years, I can tell you that the vast majority of problems my students (and I) have had at any time arose mostly because of not really paying proper attention. We THOUGHT we were paying attention, but our minds wander wander wander so much that we often don't NOTICE that though we WERE paying attention, it was to many of the wrong things - particularly in this age of endless distraction.

Love needs attention in order to be recognized, activated and increased. But in reality - fear, anxiety, regrets, worry, ruminating on past hurts, planning and scheming, doubting and manipulating, making mental lists and unmaking them - these tend to get much more attention. And since "the squeaky wheel gets the grease" we often give more attention to those who are giving us problems or who aren't loving us than to those who are right in front of us with an open heart. To really FEEL love, we have to slow down long enough to reflect upon the fruits of the loving actions we've been taking.

I realize this is a challenge. It's a challenge for me still. When I am teaching a class there may be anywhere from 15 to 600 or so people in a room with waves of love flowing back and forth between us. It's a lot to take in sometimes - and I have a LOT to DO because I usually have driven over 100 miles to get there, will have to drive 100 miles home and then still have more work to do to get the recording ready to send out. There just isn't the time or energy for me to stand and have a big love-fest at the end of the class. And there is a kind of ENERGETIC HIGH that I am on to do the traveling and channel the teaching that it is a totally different vibe than that necessary to really drink in all that wonderful liquid love. SO, though I FEEL it in the moment, I have a job to do and it's not to stand on stage and blubber because I feel so much love. HOWEVER, what I've made a practice of doing now is to sit and REFLECT on it later and to take it in fully and send it back out on an ongoing basis. In fact, this is going on with me a LOT of the time - In any given day I am usually thinking of at least a few dozen individuals whom I am appreciating and sending and receiving love with even though I have no idea where they are in time and space at that time.

Parents certainly have this experience as well. There is so much going on, so much to DO, particularly with school age kids who are constantly being driven here and there and where it's all going by so damn FAST!! Many parents FEEL the most love for their children when the kids are sound asleep and there is nothing going on or being said or done. And thought all of those things you DO are expressions and ACTIONS of love whether for others or for yourself, we also want to create space and time for the FEELINGS of love to rise up within us. So, here's another little tip to try - at the end of the day, perhaps when you crawl into bed, or even before, STOP and quietly reflect on 3 or so instances of love from the day that you want to really let into your heart and Consciousness. These can be from yourself to another, from another to you, from the Universe Itself in the form of a dazzling sunset or a soft fresh blanket of snow in the moonlight. Noticing these things and marinating in them is a radical act of self-love - but you have to slow down to the speed of love to let it catch you.

Day 27 – Look for the Beauty ONLY

One of the reasons Louise Hay is so adamant about the mirror being such a powerful tool in our healing is because it can show us where we are in terms of criticism and condemnation. What are you looking for when you look in the mirror? Many people don't even realize they are actually LOOKING for problems, issues, and things to criticize, condemn and worry about - even obsess over.

In the 1980's movie "Perfect" that was based on the then new fitness craze that's never really ended, one of the main characters was obsessed with her body, nose, cheekbones, teeth and with having plastic surgery to make herself "perfect." She believed that with perfection came love - a man who would find her desirable and worthy of his love and affection. So for her, the actual mirror became her gauge of how "lovable" she was and she was always working on fixing that image in order to be lovable. There's nothing wrong with plastic surgery or wanting to look good physically if you understand what it can and cannot do. It can give you a certain attention, but it does not make you worthy or lovable. It can even increase your confidence, but it cannot make you any more or less deserving. It's not an accomplishment.

But that is only one kind of mirror where people look for the "perfection" they believe will make them lovable. For some the mirror is their children and they must raise them as the PERFECT parent so that they will deserve love themselves. The forms of the mirror are plentiful. Some look to see their "selves" reflected in their work, their good charitable service to the world, their spiritual enlightenment, their talents and abilities, their hard work, sharp mind, strong body, helping others - believing that through these reflections they will see what makes them worthy and lovable. There is an endless inner struggle and competition to arrive at some mythical place or state through achieving SOMETHING that will take away any feelings of "not good enough" and replace them with a feeling of deservability.

But these images and the striving for perfection is actually what keeps love from being recognized or let in. We are not loved for our perfection but more often for the oddities that make us unique. In fact, it can be in our weaknesses that we are most lovable if we can let go of the myth of perfection. Sometimes what you are trying to fix and get rid of is exactly what many people find so fascinating, lovable and wonderful about you.

When we begin to look for beauty instead of focusing on our perceived obstacles to perfection, everything starts to shift. And as I always say, things can turn around to the positive very fast, just as quickly as it seems to go to hell. A rescue dog that's been unloved and abused may take a long time to physically recover, but their spirit and inner being can come along very quickly in the presence of loving care from someone who is seeing them as perfect in spite even of being very needy. Boot camp is about looking for the reflection of your beauty in all things - your work, your play, your family, your home, your personality and mind and talents and body and face and eyes and everything. Look for whatever things are good, whatever things are lovely, whatever things are of good report, even in the midst of a giant fucking mess, and you will find that you have become a true peacemaker because you are at peace with yourself.

Day 28 – Nothing is Missing From You

Many of the cultures we live in are casting an endless spell through every means possible to instill doubt within us and to have us "searching" to find what we're "missing." It's used to sell us shit and control us in various ways - whether it's about our bodies and health, our money or relationships, our future security, our spiritual development or anything else.

So, people go from thing to thing to thing, looking for the missing thing that does not exist at all. There is nothing missing from you - nothing. Every answer that you seek is already there once you ask the question within. Experts, teachers, books, and so on - all can be helpful research along the way and in providing validation, encouragement or helping us to stay awake, but they are not going to provide the "missing something" because that is just another erroneous concept.

Yes, you have made mistakes as we all do, but *you* are not a mistake. You are not insufficient. You are part of a vast expanding Universal Intelligence, at one with everything - how could anything be missing from you. There's no party going on that's more fun than where you are right now when you realize this. Now you are free to come and go, when, where and as you please, out of clear thinking and seeing instead of from any compulsion to seek outside yourself for anything lacking. Your travels are meant to be these joyous adventures in sharing with other complete beings, celebrating your wholeness.

You are not a project to be completed, or a problem to be fixed. You are not "working" your way through incarnations to get somewhere higher. Let go of all that nonsense, and you will just naturally rise up and up. Blow your own mind today by understanding that even if everyone and everything you "had" was gone tomorrow, there would still be nothing missing. Everyone and everything is here to enjoy, but none of it is our Source. Everything comes from Source and goes back to Source, over and over again in a delicious dance of Life. You already are wise - but perhaps you've fallen under the hypnotic spell again of trying to find wisdom "out there."

Call off the search.

Day 29 – Fitting In Is For Sponges

It's quite possible that you are weird. You might even be super weird. In fact, you may be in a category all by yourself - or a few decades ahead of your time. Congratulations!! You don't need to fit in everywhere. A sponge fits in everywhere and you are a Star Child, not a Porifera.

If you are weird or strange, then you may very well be marginalized by society and not given a "seat at the table." But take a look at who is sitting at the table. They're all pretty miserable and stressed out trying to impress each other and to cover up their own insecurities. It's not working.

Now, look over at the little kid's table. That's where all the fun is going on and where the real magic of manifestation comes from. They haven't forgotten about where they came from yet. They know that nothing is more real than pretending and believing. They see nothing strange about dressing up in a costume every day. They don't think there is anything they cannot be or do or have yet. It's a table full of beings with limitless possibilities. Over at the other table - beings with extremely limited belief systems. That's not your table.

You live in Opposite World, where weird is just about the best thing you can be. You're a Light-Walker and magic comes very naturally to you when you let yourself remember your Connection to the Light Source. Don't lose faith. Don't lose your wonder and belief. Your people will find you. Be patient and shine bright so they can see you. Practice your magic today. You're going to have an awesome week.

Day 30 – Get Passionate About Yourself!

Bam! You made it to day 30! You are so fucking awesome and I knew you could do it. Now, if you're not sitting down, you may want to because this entry may blow what's left of your mind. Then, take a deep breath.

Okay, ready?

<u>The meek shall not inherit the earth</u>. Not only will they inherit nothing, they are quite often mistreated all along the way to getting nothing. The meek get the shaft from the banking industry while the CEO's are off drinking champagne on their yachts. The meek are passed by for every raise and promotion. The meek are in the kitchen cleaning up while the party is in full swing in the next room. The meek turn the other cheek and end up on the fast track to crucifixion. The meek are taken advantage of all across the earth, and human history bears endless witness to this from the beginning of recorded time. There, I said it.

Sometimes religious types will try to sell you this horseshit: *"Meekness is not weakness, it's absolute strength under control."* Ignore that. Just more brainwashing to get you to sit down so they can sell you more crap and keep you asleep to who you really are. That kind of thinking is always extreme - you're either the homeowner getting the shaft or you have to be the bank taking advantage. But, that's a cartoon of life that says that the strong and bold are greedy and brutish. Get that idea out of your head. It's a spell you're under. (I believe Jesus was wildly misquoted all through scriptures anyhow - and these kinds of teachings are exactly what the early church promoted to keep the people docile and easily controllable.)

Recently I saw a few minutes of an interview on television with the adult son of a very famous wealthy ambitious businessman. He said something very spontaneous and "politically incorrect" that was both hilariously accurate and extremely telling. He said, *"My father is very passionate about himself."* I nearly spit out my water because it was so outrageously true and not the kind of public relations spin bullshit that we're used to hearing. He didn't say his father was passionate about his work, his mission, his family, his legacy - he said he was passionate about HIMSELF!

It made me laugh and then it made me REALLY think and realize how fabulous that is. I've known many successful people who were passionate about their work, mission, goals, empire and so on, but many times they were still filled with self-loathing and feelings of endlessly pushing themselves to achieve more, thinking that it would take away those feelings. It didn't and it doesn't. Plenty of people spend their lives doing wonderful things that they are very passionate about and they still die feeling inadequate and incomplete.

So it comes down to this - if YOU are not passionate about YOU, who will be? And why would they be, if YOU aren't? I'm not talking about being arrogant, or stepping on other people, or feeling superior to anyone - that's all the extremist black and white thinking that comes from having been brainwashed by religion or the culture. Because in the end, all you really have is yourself. In an instant, everything else can be gone - the mission, the career, your family and friends, your legacy. All of it can be wiped out in an instant and what you will be left to start over with is . . . YOU. You're going to be with you FOREVER and being ambivalent about yourself, being meek and wishy-washy about YOU, well it's going to suck ass. You gotta turn that shit around.

Now, this is not about getting argumentative and loud or aggressive. Remember, the most powerful shift we can ever make is in our own CONSCIOUSNESS. This is an inner shift that will begin to change your whole energy field. We replace the old meekness with an attitude of BOLDNESS. You've got to become your own biggest fan. You know who Wayne Dyer's biggest fan was? Wayne Dyer. He talked about himself endlessly in all his books and TV specials in the most glowing terms and frankly he couldn't get enough of himself. And yet, he mostly came across as a very friendly folksy father-figure type who was enjoying the fuck out of his life while helping millions of his fans through his work - but he was not meek or self-effacing. In fact, I'd say he was quite ambitious, as are most people who get anywhere in this life. And please, DO NOT equate ambition with ruthlessness - that's another EXTREMIST black and white attitude. Boldness is about speaking up, remembering that a closed mouth never gets fed.

So pat yourself on the back for making it 1/3 of the way through boot camp already! You are gaining momentum and are becoming unstoppable as you continue lining up behind yourself. The best is yet to come.

DAY 31 – LET YOUR FREAK FLAG FLY BABY!

You are an original. The Light will come through you in a way that it cannot come through anyone else. Though your Consciousness is one with the Infinite Mind, it is unique for no one has or will have exactly your experiences, ideas and perceptions. In a world of endless conformity and sameness, you came here to make your own choices and walk your own path. Do not let your light diminish - do not hide it under a bushel.

The moment you water yourself down or start changing yourself in order to be accepted, you have awakened the prostitute archetype within and are selling your soul for a meaningless life of shiny things that turn out to be cheap tinsel. No one gets to vote on you. The POWER IS IN YOU, not in the world. What the world gives to you, the world can take away. What you bring forth from within you is yours forever and will serve you well, even if the whole world rejects it and laughs at you. This is only temporary. The ones who don't get you are the ones you don't want around - they will piss on your joy every chance they get because of the uncomfortable stick up their ass. Let em go.

Happily, you are living in the best time in history for being a true original, because no matter how far out in the boondocks you may live, through these technological wonders, you can reach out across time and space and fellowship with other artists of the soul. When others think you are too much, your people will shout "MORE, MORE, MORE!!" But ONLY if you stay on your own path and ignore whatever is not on it. Keep going. Rest when you need to, but then, get going again.

Ultimately, it's your CONSCIOUSNESS that is going to attract your right life to you - but not if you're not being who you are every chance you get. You may be in a position where you need to be buttoned down in a suit 40 or so hours a week and sitting in a cubicle staring at a screen - all the while feeling that this is NOT you. It's fine, as long as when you get home you can put on your "you" outfit and play your guitar in the garage, or work on your painting in a corner of the living room on the weekends, or write your erotic fiction during lunches, or whatever it is that helps you find your voice and use it in the ways that are the most satisfying to YOU. What satisfies YOU will be a vibration that will resound across the ethers to reach those who have been searching for you. There's nothing more insane than trying to reach the MAXIMUM amount of people or trying to appeal to a "broader audience" - an artist of the soul has no time for that bullshit. Take a good look at what is most popular and remember that shit draws flies - LOTS of them. And if you do attract the masses, it will be because the world finally caught up with you.

What you want is to appeal to the people on YOUR frequency. Don't make them wait. Don't sit down and shut up. Make a joyous noise, even if others call is noise pollution. Rock and roll was thought of as vulgar and course at one time and Elvis Presley was filmed on TV from the waist up because of his gyrating hips. You don't need to be an Elvis, just be you full out.

Day 32 – You Are Programmed for Impossible

You are an Infinite Being who came here from the Limitless in order to evolve your Light in wonderful joyous ways. You did not come here to suss out what you think you might be able to do given your age, background, intelligence and talents, the current economy and where you live and so on. You did not come to be reasonable. You were not programmed for reasonable and safe. You were programmed by the Light to regularly achieve the seemingly impossible - because it is so much fucking fun and it lights the way for those coming up behind you.

Everything is about Consciousness, and frankly, Consciousness is either blocked or allowed by your own SELF-PERCEPTION. It's not merely what you think is possible in general - more specifically; it is what YOU THINK IS POSSIBLE FOR YOU! Today is your day. Now is your time. Every day. All the time. You've got what it takes. It was programmed into you at the Source. Your job is to ACTIVATE "it." And "it" gets activated by your desires, by what you want, whether it is for yourself, another person, or the world - whether it is physical and tangible or an experience, feeling or state of being.

Take that desire and add IMAGINATION to it, and you've ACTIVATED the Source Program. Now to RUN the program, you start adding BELIEF - belief that it's possible, that it's possible FOR YOU, that whatever you need to accomplish your desire is even now starting to sparkle and jump and come to LIFE because it FEELS you calling it with your Consciousness.

This shit is big. Massive. Get on board with your fine self. Impossible things are happening every day. Diseases that used to kill are being managed and even healed. People are dreaming new dreams at 70, 80 and 90 years of age. Country bumpkins even manage their fears and go on the world stage. Come hear the music play - nothing is impossible except in a limiting story we tell ourselves.

DAY 33 – BE GENTLE

Today's boot camp lesson and exercise is so simple that it can easily be passed over - yet it is the deepest of any of the lessons we will cover here. The only way for you to truly receive the full benefit of it is to take it on as a kind of living meditation and contemplation that only BEGINS today and carries you through the rest of the 90 days. It is simply this: <u>Be Gentle With Yourself</u>.

Do NOT add anything to this at all. Don't add anything about doing battle or how hard it is or any embellishment or dramatization of it. Leave it be as it is in simple elegance - eat it, breathe it, drink it, sleep in it, walk in it, rest in it. Write it on 100 post-its and make it your screensaver. Let it carry you through the next 57 days and beyond. It is enough.

DAY 34 – AWAKEN FROM THE TRANCE

The big not-so-secret thing about life on this planet is that human beings LOVE to terrify themselves. Actually, the better life on the earth gets, the more Dystopian movies get made. There really are no Utopian movies being made. You wouldn't know it from TV or the internet, but life keeps getting better all the time, which is NOT to say there aren't major problems - only that things are so WILDLY better than they've ever been close to being, ever. Child mortality rates, curing diseases, gay marriage, an African American president, how easy it is to run our daily lives compared to days of washboards and ice boxes, and on and on. It's amazing how many people living in a near Utopia are sitting around imagining and visualizing a desolate and horrible future for society and the world. There are people who actually spend a large part of their time and energy SEEKING OUT bad news and things that will disturb them. They are extremely annoyed by people who are peaceful and happy because they think them as ignorant and uninformed.

Yes, people go out of their way to terrify themselves. A family goes off on a wonderful camping trip, and the first night - ghost stories or tales of a man with a hook for a hand! Our children are told "fairy tales" about a wicked queen who wants a hunter to cut the heart out of a pretty maiden and bring it to her in a box. I was read "Beautiful Bible Stories" in bed at night about King Solomon ordering a baby to be cut in half and of God ordering Abraham to KILL his son Isaac as a blood sacrifice to him, which turned out to be just a test, ha ha! And then I said a prayer I was taught that included the line - *"If I should DIE before I wake!!"* HUH? We LOVE to terrify ourselves and our children so much that we don't even realize we're doing it most of the time. People like to jump out of planes, go on wild roller coasters, swim with sharks, and watch the plethora of TV shows and movies about serial killers, monsters, zombies and demons. Many terrify themselves with visions of a burning hell to come, the Apocalypse, an angry God, evil loosed in the world and on and on.

If all else fails, there is simply tossing and turning in bed all night worrying about getting sick, not having money for retirement, not having the right body, ending up alone, wondering how our kids will turn out, obsessing over looking stupid or foolish, imagining yourself in all kinds of horrible scenarios, wondering if your dreams will ever come true or if you'll reach your goals, feeling guilty about what you think you should or shouldn't be doing - well, you get the picture. It's a hypnotic trance, a kind of spell. *"Light came into the world, but men preferred darkness"* is just as true today . . . and that fact makes it very simple to sell us everything from lipstick to insurance policies to bibles to underground bunkers to psychic protection smudge sticks. I'm not against any of these. What I'm trying to do is help you wake up to remembering that there are not two powers at work in the world. There is only one power and one Presence.

It's all the endless trance of the world to keep people convinced that they are powerless in a very dangerous world that is out to get them. Terrifying yourself this way is the extreme opposite of self-love - it is self-torment to the extreme. I know, I did it so well for years that I had panic attacks all through my childhood and would even break out from head to toe in hives from anxiety. My very first wake up call from the trance was back in the very early 1970's when a female doctor (Rare in rural Pennsylvania at the time, plus she was Indian – I adored her.) told my parents while I was standing right next to them, *"Is he worried a lot, because this is all in his head"* about some weird symptom I had come in with again. I was literally making myself sick all the time - an attack on self from the inside. I think of that doctor as an angel from some other dimension who came to set me off on the right path. After that day, I began reading a book on self-hypnosis to learn how to use my mind to calm me down. That was 8 million years ago and I still use the same techniques today but with much more skill and experience, to calm and center myself to this very day.

Remember, when it comes to the fear that most people reading this face on a daily basis, "THE CALLS ARE COMING FROM INSIDE THE HOUSE" is more true than that the fear is coming from outside of us. The opposite is also very true. The POWER is inside of us - not out there. It takes the diligence of a Soldier of Light to stay alert and it basically comes down to a habit of QUESTIONING EVERYTHING ALL THE TIME. Don't believe everything you hear, read or think. Investigate for yourself. See how it feels. Look for evidence of what you WANT instead of what you DO NOT want. Being awake feels so fucking awesome because it feels so ordinary in the best way imaginable. It feels like being alert, walking around in the normal world without clinging or aversion - basically without fear. Being gentle with yourself means NO LONGER terrifying yourself unless you are doing it on purpose because you want to for fun - like watching a scary movie, or riding the biggest roller coaster in the park. Do not let yourself fall under the spell for long. Never be complicit in your own mental torture. This is how we progress - we don't wake up once and for all, but with practice we stay awake for longer and longer periods of time.

DAY 35 – GET OVER YOURSELF

A while back, mogul Oprah Winfrey bought 10% of Weight Watchers stock. She revealed on the Ellen DeGeneres talk show that she'd joined WW briefly many years ago, maybe for a day or two before giving it up. She didn't want to count points. Something about it bugged her. Apparently, at that time she preferred running a marathon to counting points. That's what we call "resistance." We have a goal, something we want or want to do or be or experience, and immediately we are met with our own inner resistance to DOING this or that. It's what one teacher calls, "the will to fail" which is talking ourselves out of something before we even really get started. We fail on the sofa instead of in the actual game. We talk ourselves out of it instead of facing and walking through our resistance.

As a kid I loved to swim, but I very rarely did even though I went to the local pool all the time. In rural Pennsylvania the public pool was filled with spring water from the mountains and that water was freezing cold even on the hottest days. The creek in back of our house was the same. A bulldozer would come each summer to dig out the creek deep enough for us to be able to swim in, but I mostly sat along the side watching everyone else swim. I wanted to swim without getting wet or cold or taking off my shirt because I was embarrassed by my scrawny body. That's resistance to living the life we want. Let's not fall into the "spiritual" trap of calling it fear. It's resistance.

Oprah told Ellen that since sometime in August, she has lost 15 pounds on Weight Watchers by counting points. She had to get over herself, <u>as we all do our entire lives</u> every time resistance comes up to stop us from going forward toward our goals and dreams. This is a major part of self-love, encouraging and even pushing yourself to go past the resistance that keeps you from going for it in life - particularly as we age and have more past experiences of pain or failure to use as the excuse to not try - the will to fail can get much worse if we are not careful and alert to the pattern.

Can you imagine how much harder it was for Oprah to train for and run an entire marathon than to just count points and learn about portion size? But many times in life we go waaaaaaaay the long hard complicated way around something in order to KEEP our resistance intact - to NOT have to change, to NOT press through the fear - even someone like Oprah who has done so much and tried everything under the sun has resistance which can keep her stuck in an old pattern. It's nothing to be ashamed of, but it's also nothing to lie to ourselves about.

You'd think it would be only about big scary things - but we can talk ourselves out of doing FUN things like going to a party, or an art showing, or a play just 5 minutes after we just told someone how much we want to make new friends and expand our social circle. It's THE WILL TO FAIL when we talk ourselves out of leaving our suffocating comfort zone. So, it can be very good self talk at times like this to say, *"Jacob, get over yourself. Go do the thing you don't want to do - do it as an act of self-love. Don't be so fucking stubborn. Go for what you want. Keep breathing and don't stop moving forward. No one is stopping you but you. You CAN do this."* I'm getting SO MUCH better now at seeing how it's only my resistance that keeps me from living more fully. I keep busting myself when I am making VALID EXCUSES which are really nothing more than me giving in to my own internal resistance and not wanting to be uncomfortable or rejected or to experience loss. The way to get over resistance is to see it for what it is and gently press on through it one step at a time, as an act of self-love.

DAY 36 – GIVE UP ALTRUISM

It's amazing how many altruistic types I know who either suffer from deep depression or a whole cavalcade of chronic illnesses or serious weight issues (under or over). That's because altruism unnatural and stupid. Preferring others to yourself or practicing selflessness is another religious spiritual bs move that really is the opposite of the Universal plan for our good. In fact, those altruistic types who are always putting others first then often end up so sick that they need others to take care of them later. It's an unnecessary cycle and totally unnatural even spiritually.

The thing to do is drop altruism and instead <u>awaken the NATURAL tendency of humans toward benevolence.</u> Altruism is preferring others to self and putting them first - and it involves personal sacrifice. <u>Benevolence is the **desire** to do good to others, it is based on goodwill, which is natural to humans.</u> People are naturally good though this is seldom believed because we've been brainwashed to believe otherwise. YOU are naturally and inherently good. You do not need to be guilted into helping others and it is not necessary to sacrifice to do so. Benevolence has no "should" vibration to it, nor any sense that others should be doing it too. It's based on freedom and generosity of spirit. And while you're at it, let go of the concept of "service" too. Service is another one of those things that is unnatural. <u>Just help.</u> Service has the vibration of INEQUALITY someone higher up helping someone lower down, or the lower ranks are serving the King and Queen. Therefore, it's also self-sacrificing and wrong-headed. <u>Help happens among equals, though the equality has nothing to do with form – we are</u>

equal as extensions of God-Source. We help someone now; we'll need help later. We're all equals who are not "serving" but we understand that EVERYONE needs help and we enjoy helping whenever we can. We're not serving the homeless - we're helping that man over there who needs some help today. Tomorrow we may need someone to help us move but we're not going to ask our friends if they'd like to come "serve us" this weekend. Get real.

In fact, the only people who've ever really been cheap and miserly with me are the altruistic service-oriented types. This is because they are so brainwashed into upside down thinking that their relationship to giving and receiving is the extreme opposite of reality. It is based on guilt and shame, both felt and projected.

Let it go. Altruism is a kind of shameful guilty self-attack. Instead, change your self-concept to one of a benevolent successful thriving human being who gives from abundance and goodwill rather than from any sense of owing something to the world or humanity. You are much bigger than that.

DAY 37 – DON'T BE AFRAID TO BE A LITTLE PUSHY

There's a difference between being pushy and being obnoxious. I'm not talking about being aggressive or getting in someone's face or losing your pleasant demeanor. But sometimes people can be too passive about going after what they want and they turn tail and run before the person in front of them has gotten to the end of the word "no."

Really it's about persistence, but the more passive types will think of it as being pushy to keep jumping hurdles and knocking on doors if it doesn't work right away. Keep going. Don't give up. And don't take anything personally. <u>You DESERVE and have a right to ask for what you want and to keep on asking for it</u>. No one is going to do it for you. And many of the people I know who keep achieving their goals and dreams are those that I used to think of as "too pushy" - until I realized they got results while I was still sitting on the sidelines politely waiting my turn . . . which never comes when you've put yourself on the bench.

BUT, in those times and situations where I pushed through my resistance to seeming "pushy" and persisted, it's almost always led to something good even if it wasn't the thing that I was going after at the time. I can't tell you how many times someone told me no - but if they stayed engaged in the conversation, they usually ended up saying yes and it all turned out wonderfully. A lot of my success in life has come simply from the fact that I was the only one who was still showing up long after everyone else had given up and gone home. Even now, the only areas of my life where I still am not truly thriving are the ones in which I give up too easily or take a "no" personally. I'm working through it and the work is exciting when I pay attention to the little and sometimes big signs of growth and forward movement.

It's finding the balance of maintaining a soft open heart but having a thick skin. We all get knocked down a lot in a lifetime - don't let it shut you down. Get used to rejection and wear it as a badge of honor that proves you're still showing up for life and your yes is probably right around the next corner.

DAY 38 – WHAT DO YOU WANT?

For many years I kept journals. My journals were not the fascinating kind full of juicy stories of my adventurous life, nor even filled with bad poetry and the deep feelings that arose within me from the loss of so many loved ones over the years. They were basically volumes of me whining - and you wouldn't really have seen much difference between a journal written when I was 22 than one written when I was 40. When I realized this, I burned them all and stopped keeping a journal. I thought I was at the very least "venting" my feelings by getting them all out on paper. I hadn't yet quite realized I was merely ACTIVATING those feelings over and over, day after day, week after week, decade after decade. Whatever we focus on, we just keep focusing on and seeing more of and for many of us that focus is on what we DO NOT WANT. So, we just keep living in an atmosphere of what we do not want. Thoughts do not leave their source.

NOW, my daily writing is usually just about two things - what I am grateful for (what IS working), and what I want to see or feel or experience in my world. And when I DO need to vent feelings that are painful or stressful I realize that is only HALF the process. I will write them all out on paper in the most raw unenlightened way possible - all the blame, guilt, anger, hopelessness, pain and so on. Then, when that's out I go on to the REALLY IMPORTANT part - I write down how I NOW WANT TO FEEL instead. This is how I reset the inner GPS system. All my years of "venting" my dark feelings on paper was continually setting the GPS to that exact same destination day after day after day. Hope does not set the GPS. AND the great thing is that you do no have to know HOW you are going to feel the way you want! WORDS are containers for power and if we ruminate on them and keep them in front of us, the subconscious mind begins to move us in that direction almost automatically.

I have post-it's in my car and home that read, *"So what DO you want?"* as a way to bring me back onto the highlighted route to my emotional well being and my cork bobbing in joy again. You might be surprised how helpful a simple little thing like this can be because if I don't pay attention my mind can be consumed with what I don't want, *"I hope there's no traffic. I hope she isn't there. My leg hurts. I'm behind this week already. I probably should have done that differently. It's taking too long to get in shape, it's probably not really working at all."* and on and on. With just a little reminder of "so, what DO you want?" my mind is turned a total 180 degrees to going in the RIGHT direction instead of continuing on going down, down, down.

We have a choice of whether we will mentally torture ourselves, or soothe ourselves. One is not very loving, one is. Choose deliberately.

Day 39 – Take Pride

You are a creation of the limitless Universal Source, the Great Spirit. What is there to be humble about? Being self-effacing and demure is unnatural and is part of the brainwashing of the world. Be natural instead of falsely humble just because you were taught that's somehow cool or more spiritual. Be proud. Be happy to have been created so magnificently by a Power that creates worlds. I don't mean arrogance - you are not better than any other creation, but then comparison and competition are the road to misery anyhow. Take pride in yourself as this glorious creation in order to HONOR the Great Spirit which you are an extension of by holding your head up high and knowing that you are as important and valuable as any other living creature on the Earth. Do it as an homage to Source.

Then, let that extend to what YOU create. Take pride in your creations. Be deliberate and focused with your energy and intention when it really counts. Step up your game from time to time. Don't get lazy and sloppy or get away with what you can because THIS will chip away at your own feelings of self-esteem.

There was a TV show I loved called, "Tabatha's Salon Takeover" which was a reality show in which Tabatha would come to a beauty salon that was just about to go under financially and she would kick the asses of everyone there who was asleep at the wheel. What fascinated me was that in every show there would be one person who HAAAAAATED Tabatha the most and it was always the one who was doing the least and fucking up the most - skating by, partying too much, being late for appointments, doing shoddy work, dressing badly, not keeping a clean station, drinking while cutting hair and on and on with TONS of justifications and excuses. Now, these are actually all signs of low self worth even though the person would insist they "didn't care" what Tabatha had to say and that they were very happy before she showed up.

And so many times, by the end of the show, THAT would be the person who adored Tabatha the most! She had told them to get their shit together or they were fired from the salon - period. And IF they actually DID what she said, usually very reluctantly, it began to change them. Once they were really bringing their A game and taking pride in their work - IT MADE THEM FEEL GOOD ABOUT THEMSELVES! When they were half-assing it and phoning it in, it was part of the vicious cycle that kept them feeling bad about themselves, their work, and everything else. You could actually see a LIGHT inside of them that had switched on - that light was pride in themselves.

If you've been working hard, instead of whining and complaining about it as so many do, step back and feel GOOD about yourself and what you are creating! Let your creations bring you MORE joy. There was a special on PBS I watched titled, "Inside Claridge's" about a beautiful old Art Deco (my favorite) 5 star luxury hotel in London that's been there since 1856 - basically it was about the staff there, many of whom have been there for 20 or 30 or more years. It was about the pride they have in doing their jobs and how much joy it brings them. They were training a new waiter on how to set up the room service cart - how everything lines up

EXACTLY, and this should be one inch from that, and so on. Fabulous! It reminded me of Downton Abbey, or even Martha Stewart when she is teaching something. The work is precise, very busy, lots going on, but they were not complaining - they had a PRIDE IN THEMSELVES and in their work.

I always LOVE setting up the room before a class - there is something so ZEN about preparing the energy for everyone to come by rearranging the chairs, lighting the candles, setting up the music, bringing the tablecloth and books and so on. I take pride in doing that all a very certain way and it makes ME feel good about myself to do it well. <u>Take pride and take credit</u> for what you've accomplished and done even if not another living soul ever notices. There is nothing wrong with tooting your own horn from time to time.

DAY 40 – BE PATIENT WITH YOURSELF

It's good to remember this is a journey of progress, not perfection. Additionally, it is not a race. Self-love is not a destination or goal that you will arrive at one day. This is a journey of the soul that will continue on til the day you leave this realm. We make good progress but can then fall down and backslide at times. It's okay. You're okay. Don't give up on yourself. Encourage yourself and remember to be on YOUR team no matter what.

This is not about psyching yourself up all the time with ultra positive self talk, though that can be part of it at times. Quite a bit of it is also about quietly accepting where you are and recognizing your steps forward no matter how seemingly small they may be. Don't get into black-and-white all-or-nothing thinking. You're doing great and your journey is not to be compared with some mental fantasy of perfection of where you think you should be. Slow gentle progress is usually easier to sustain and maintain anyhow.

Day 41 – Walk It Off

My friend Zan's dearly departed dog Delilah had arthritis for the last years of her life and she needed to be walked to make sure she didn't get too stiff and sore to move at all. Of course it would take a little bit before her joints would get warmed up and during that time Zan would kind of sing to her this little chant, *"walk it off, walk it off, walk it off"* to encourage and soothe Delilah. Zan is a born soother.

Well, not only did it work like magic on Delilah, many of us in class took on the exact same little chant as our own mantra as a way of getting past the things that would try to stop us in our tracks. Coaches have been telling their athletes to do this forever, but it's quite amazing how effective it is in so many other situations as well. Maybe you get annoyed at someone at work, your spouse snaps at you and your feelings are hurt, someone doesn't text you back, or any number of the little things that come up during a day to pull us down into feelings of unworthiness or guilt or shame or whatever . . . if you can, just walk it off, walk it off, walk it off. Don't carry all those grievances and resentments and bad feelings with you - ducks shake it off, people can walk it off. It's not the answer for huge issues that arise, but frankly most of the things that fuck up our lives are the million little things that we don't let go of that we don't even realize are building up and building up because we haven't released them.

This is also one of the reasons that I've often prescribed to students that if possible they take a 20-minute walk every day outside. It's a perfect opportunity to walk off any vibrations of the day that do not feel good while you walk yourself INTO a better feeling place.

DAY 42 – WHO DO <u>YOU</u> THINK YOU ARE?

Many of us heard this at various times in our life in one way or another whether from our family, school, teachers, or even the nameless voice of the culture echoing through our mind. It can come in various forms: *Who do you think you are? Don't get too big for your britches! Don't forget where you came from! Don't let it go to your head!*

It really doesn't matter who said it or whether their motivations were well meaning or vicious because the ultimately it's done to somehow keep us down instead of lifting us up. And really it doesn't matter who said because all that matters is whether we allow it to cause us to keep ourselves down by listening to that nonsense.

However, it actually IS an AWESOME question that should be asked and answered as frequently as necessary - *who <u>do</u> YOU think you are?* This is not about who you think you should be, or what you DO for work - it's not about justifying your place on earth through your hard work and struggle. Who do you think you are? What do you believe ABOUT yourself as a being, an individual apart from the collective - what do you believe is possible for you? Do you keep yourself small and your dreams tiny so that no one can ever say that you are too full of yourself, or are a dreamer, or are unrealistic and full of pipe dreams? Are you still trying to prove yourself to someone or something rather than simply following your goals because they are joyful without giving a fuck what anyone else says or thinks about it?

Who do you think you are? YOU get to decide. You are the authority of who you are. You are creating yourself by the story you tell about YOU. Be the star of your own movie, not an extra holding up the scenery - unless THAT brings you joy in which case you should play extra and hold up that scenery like nobody's business. You get to decide. You are the author of your story.

Day 43 – People Either Like You or They Don't

Trying to earn the approval, love or companionship of another person is a very special kind of hell to live in - it is 100% hopeless and futile. People either like you or the don't, they either get you or they don't, they either love you or they don't - period. If they do, awesome. If they don't, let em go and move the fuck on. No grudges or hard feelings. Your good is elsewhere and you should go to it quickly.

There is very little that will crush a sense of self worth and esteem than the humiliating and soul-crushing tap dancing routine that many people go through trying to make a relationship work when someone just doesn't see how fabulous you are already. Relationships are challenging enough when trying to negotiate our varying viewpoints about everyday things without adding the anvil of endlessly auditioning for the relationship, whether it is romantic, business, friendship or any other kind. This is not to say that we shouldn't make an effort in relationships - the problem is when we start to try to change who we are in order to make someone else happy or satisfied. It will not end well.

You're either a vibrational match or not. Focus your energy and attention on the ones who already get you and can see how awesome you are. THIS is a HUGE sign of self-love in action.

DAY 44 – YOU ARE OKAY. YOU'LL BE OKAY.

ALL power, wisdom and Presence resides in YOU, right now and always. There is a still small Voice within you, available at all times, which is quite gentle yet firm when turned to. Spending time worrying about the future is simply creating a miserable present, which you will still be living in if you don't discipline yourself to STOP - to listen to that still small Voice on a regular daily basis.

Ask that still small Voice about your future - it will <u>never</u> say, *"Man, you are fucked! There's nothing but bedlam, misery and decline ahead for you!"* Instead, it will tell you how fabulous you are and how bright your future is if you just keep going. That Voice is the SOURCE of your self-love. Remember to *"judge not according to appearances"* because the appearances are nothing more than the evidence of OLD thoughts - change the thinking and the appearances begin to shift in your perception of how you see them. The big boogeyman is seen to be nothing but a shadow. The future is a friend to us when we are thinking correctly because life is meant to get better and better as we go, not worse and more diminished. Life doesn't give up on us, but many people unconsciously retreat and give up on life out of fear.

You are okay. You will be okay. It's okay. Never stop speaking to that fabulous teenager within about the glorious future that still is ahead of you - even if your body is 90. I'd much rather speak to a youthful 90 year old than an ancient 40 year old. Just because life can be scary doesn't mean you can't enjoy the thrill of not knowing what's going to happen next instead of worrying yourself into paralysis. NO ONE knows what's going to happen next - ever. Get used to it and relax into the thrill of not knowing. Just keep remembering, you're okay no matter what. There is always help, always a solution - but you cannot find it in a state of panic. Tune in to that Voice and ask for Guidance - then LISTEN from a place of DEEP RELAXATION. You will find that the most amazing things can seemingly come out of nowhere when you ASK and LISTEN.

DAY 45 – CONGRATULATIONS!

You are halfway through Boot Camp! How do you feel? This is an excellent time to take stock of the progress you've made and to acknowledge yourself even if the only thing you've done is read these entries every day. Remember, there is NO WAY to lose with this. You cannot "fail" this boot camp, so if you think you've fucked up at all, shred that evidence and retain only whatever it may have taught you about loving yourself more unconditionally.

How has your self-talk been? Are you being kinder to yourself? Has it rippled out to others? Are you taking certain actions more frequently that make your life better whether with your body, relationships, work, etc.? Are you terrifying yourself less, giving yourself a break more regularly, showing up for yourself more?

The halfway mark is a good time to reflect on where you are and to see if you want to make some course corrections, recommit, pat yourself on the back, and generally give yourself a little Team celebration for being so unfailingly awesome!

DAY 46 – BE A DREAMER!
GET YOUR HEAD IN THE CLOUDS!

If you continue to follow your own path, this path of self-love and self expression, I cannot make any promises of what you will "have" other than an authentic life that is truly yours. It may not make your family proud of you and you may not make a name for yourself, but you may find that your name means more to you than it would have had you not followed your inner call. Perhaps you won't even find a place in the world, but you'll discover that you are creating your own world just as magically as you did when you were a small child.

It doesn't mean you won't be able to pay your bills, or that you'll be irresponsible and disconnected or disenfranchised either. As you know, you can have your head in the clouds while keeping your feet on solid ground. In fact, most of the early scientists were dreamers, living in a world of imagination. Insisting that science and imagination are separate is the opposite of progress. True invention is born in the minds and hearts of those who are willing to create a different world in imagination first - this is the site of first creation whether the creation is a great story, piece of music, technology, medicine or a new theory of how the universe operates.

Being a dreamer, having your head in the clouds . . . well, you can still have a very intense corporate job or spend your days doing something which is mindlessly repetitive, but you will not simply be another drone hypnotized by the culture into buying into a lifestyle instead of creating a life. There is a part of you that will keep exploring and believing, creating and growing regardless of what your life "looks like" on the outside. You'll see that all the people who told you to stop being a dreamer and to get your head out of the clouds were simply afraid for you, afraid for themselves. And though your body will continue to experience time and space, you will find that you are ageless and timeless and without limit. No matter what perceived physical limits you may have, your spirit will roam freely throughout the ever-expanding multiverse of infinite potential. If someone calls you a dreamer with your head in the clouds, take the compliment - you are in amazing company.

DAY 47 – MAKE GOOD CHOICES

One morning at the Starbucks in West Hollywood, a young man walked in looking somewhat like a sexy pirate. He seemed to know a lot of the people working behind the counter and he exuded a kind of relaxed yet outgoing joy. There was a lot of fun chatter going on with he and everyone around him and then as he was walking out the door with his coffee (and this is a very LARGE Starbucks), he shouted across the room to his friends behind the counter, *"See you later. Make good choices!"* This funny reminder made my whole day. What a delightfully funny way to encourage self-love and care. Such simplicity.

You know those choices you make that sabotage your goals, make you feel bad, disturb your inner peace and take you in the wrong direction? Don't do that today. You know those choices you make that support your goals and self-esteem, make you feel good about yourself and life and take you in the right direction? Do that today.

So often we complicate things with our thinking and then we call it complicated. Most things are really very simple if we will just remove our STORY around it all and ALLOW it to be simple. Make good choices. So simple. Do that today and see what happens and how you feel at the end of the day. And then keep doing it until it becomes a habit. And when you fall down or fuck up, which happens, forgive yourself immediately and get right back on the highlighted route of making good choices.

DAY 48 – THINK LOVE AND JOY

This is the best beauty treatment you will ever give yourself and all the members of your team will love it and be deeply served by it - body, mind, heart and spirit. I find this to be an even better practice than gratitude and appreciation.

It's very simple and you can do it most any time and any place. Simply let your mind drift to what you love and what brings you joy. If you helps you can write it down but it's not necessary - do whatever feels best and most effective. Really marinate in the feelings and visions of what you love and what brings you joy, what makes your heart sing. If you are alone you can even talk to yourself about what it is about these people, places and things that you love or that makes you feel so joyful.

This is not about yearning or wanting or desiring, it's not about grief or longing for what was or might have been. This is not about sentiment - it's about chewing and reflecting on what you really love to do, see, feel, taste, think of, be with, or experience, and most of it will probably be very simple ordinary things like sunsets and hot muffins and kitten lips and the smell of a baby's head - but don't limit yourself in any way because it can also be flying first class to Paris. Focus on all that brings joy to your life, even if it's something you've never done or somewhere you've never been but you just FEEL JOY when you think about it or see photos or hear someone talk about it.

People spend at least this much time torturing themselves imagining all the things they hope don't happen, or worrying about this or that, and that is quite often things that have nothing to do with them that they cannot do anything about. This love and joy exercise is a way to LOVE and soothe yourself every day instead of terrifying yourself. You're not trying to manifest or create a single thing here - this is about an inner daily massage for your whole team. Try working this into conversations - start kicking off new topics with, *"You know what I love . . . "* and then fill in the blank and see if you can steer everyone into talking about what they love too. It's much better than 99% of the conversations that go on most of the time and you will be getting your valve soooo open to let in more good.

DAY 49 – YOU ARE AMAZING!

Receive that. Right now. You may not have heard it this week, or month, or century - so I'm letting you know right now. It's possible it's not been noticed, but even more possible that it's been noticed and someone MEANT to let you know, but then got all caught up in life and they forgot.

I know all that you do and how hard you work to make a difference, to be there, to help and to contribute - and that it is often not seen or acknowledged. But I'm acknowledging it now. But more importantly YOU must acknowledge it and KNOW what you did. Let it help you sleep soundly at night knowing that you did your part, little or small - some days bigger, some days smaller.

Don't forget, boot camp is about GETTING ON YOUR OWN TEAM. Root for yourself. You're making wonderful progress. You matter. You count. Even a smile you share may be the very thing that gives someone the hope to go on another day. Your part is important. Play it like it's the lead even if you are the only one in the theater.

Day 50 – "I Always Have What I Need."

I really want to drum this one into both your conscious and subconscious mind as fully as I can because it may be one of the most loving things that you can ever do for yourself. I keep reminding you that the fatal flaw most of us have when it comes to self-love are all the ways we worry and torment ourselves needlessly (as if there is ever a need to torment ourselves).

Put this thought at the top of your list for the rest of this boot camp as a "go to" thought to use to counteract any thoughts of scarcity, fear and limitation that may arise during the week - as well as those times when you might have a tendency to feel like you have to micromanage, control, struggle, work hard and do everything yourself.

No matter what confronts you this week, no matter how minor, simply let your first thought be, *"It's okay, I always have what I need"* and you might even imagine that you are plugging yourself into the Universal Power Supply the way that you plug your phone in to be charged every night. When we say to ourselves, *"I always have what I need"* it's not because of our own individual strength or wisdom but rather that we are plugged into INFINITE POWER and WISDOM from which EVERYTHING COMES. We do not have to MAKE anything happen because we are plugged into the Source and are getting out of our own way!

DAY 51 – FORGET YOUR AGE

That's right. Just let it slip your mind entirely. Forget about all the nonsense of "acting your age" and the other things the culture says to try to shame and control you. If you are living according to the boxes that society tries to put us in, there are probably only about 5 "good years" in a life when you are not too young to do this or that, or too old to do this or that. What rubbish.

I know a very active and happy "older" couple who tell people they have no idea how old they are. If you ask them, they just say, *"I'm not sure. I forget."* They say they can't even remember the year they were born. You'd be surprised how much that pisses some people off - particularly doctors. People hate not being able to silently judge and predict your eventual decline. But we don't have to decline if we refuse to accept the social boxes.

There are tribes of people on this earth in which the members actually have NO idea how old they are. They don't count the passing of time. They live in the now and so there's no reverence for old people, nor are they discarded and pushed aside because of age. Everyone is equal and active - fully engaged in living each day without placing a value on a number of years. Isn't that fabulous?

You can actually decide not to participate in the limits of the age game. Stop talking about it and ruminating on it. Let it go. It's meaningless. Stop thinking about retirement and fixed incomes - think about freedom and new adventures instead. Forget about being part of a particular "generation" -

that's all made up nonsense and has NOTHING to do with you. There's no such thing as a generation. It's just another limiting box that society tries to jam us into. You can opt out of it if you choose.

ALL things are possible for those who live beyond the false limits and restrictions of the society and culture. Set yourself free and forget about the illusory passage of time. You'll enjoy life a lot more and you might even find yourself playing more as you lose yourself in the joy of the present.

DAY 52 – MAKE PEACE WITH WHERE YOU ARE

Making peace with where you are and with what is currently happening in your life does not mean you have to remain there. But waging war and resisting the present is a very unkind thing to do to yourself and will stress you out. It is shitting on your now. And since what we resist tends to persist, it also isn't very helpful. The more we resist, the longer it will FEEL like everything is taking.

We can work to make changes while making the best of the present and it is a much kinder to ourselves to find something, anything, to be grateful for and to appreciate while we move forward. If it is possible to very quickly make a positive change in a way that is not harmful, go for it. But quite often it takes some time and planning - and while that process is going on, it will usually feel much better if you are soothing yourself and practicing appreciation than if you are bitching and moaning all the time.

Make yourself FEEL GOOD today rather than increasing what feels bad. Spend as much time as possible focusing on what there is to appreciate - talk about it, amplify it, thank and praise it, for your own sake. Make peace with your now AND keep taking positive actions to change whatever you want to change.

DAY 53 – INVOKING THE NEW WORLD

Here's another outrageous Truth that will set you free if you can begin to embrace it. It is another slice of the terrible swift sword that cuts through the delusions and bondage of the old world of suffering and sacrifice. It is this - remembering and commemorating the horrors of the past do not stop them from happening again. In fact, they create the vibrational frequency which has kept them happening since the birth of recorded time. And continually grieving over what has been lost, what no longer is, what has changed, and what used to be better - well, it just makes a person ugly and rigid. Adapting and evolving not only technologically but also emotionally and mentally is what keeps a person from becoming a dinosaur that is forever clinging to the "good old days" of classic cars and the old architecture that just reproduced ages gone by. People forget those were the "good old days" of segregation, polio, women unable to vote, hand laundering everything, no recycling anything, dense smog, high childhood mortality, no penicillin, blood-letting and so many other "old-fashioned delights."

The new world comes only when we are willing to update the old wine skins and create NEW wine skin paradigms by looking forward, not back. Lot's wife was turned to a pillar of salt because of looking back at the ruin and grief behind her and humanity does the same thing day after day after day. You will never meet a truly happy or interesting person who is always talking and thinking about the past. Nothing is deader than the past. Let the dead bury the dead. *"He is not a God of the dead, but of the living"* is still true today. It's not about discarding the past or forgetting it - but it IS about putting it in the past to focus on the NOW and the joy of what lies ahead.

The new world is already here every moment that one is willing to summon it - and that happens by letting go of your ideas of how things are supposed to be or look. It is experienced by letting go of trying to create something new out of old paradigms. There is a new world which already exists for many in which gender and sexuality are fluid - in which "old" and "young" join together because of vibrational matching and not because of generational likeness - in which stability is not based on something you own or have - in which business is not based on bricks and mortar - in which prosperity is not based on only dollars - in which sanity is not based on conformity to a norm - in which family is not about roles being played - oh, and so much more. It is not a "new world order" because it has too much individual freedom for anything so corny and outdated. The old world will continue to exist right next to the new one because it will be held there by the consciousness of those who prefer bondage and good old fashioned mental slavery.

It's not that change is a comin' - it's already and forever here for those who choose not to give in to the illusory comfort and seeming "safety" of bondage and oppression from the culture. The new world has just as much comfort, luxury and so much more than the old world. But it does mean a constant letting go and opening the mind to NEW energy, new ideas, and new ways of being. It's scary and thrilling and is the true fountain of youth. In the new world there's a lack of boxes to check on forms. Who you are cannot be checked off on a form - and that enrages the culture that needs to put everything in a nice neat category. What the young have to learn from the old is not about history and how things used to be but rather about what it takes to navigate through life, to absorb loss and keep on finding joy in life. What the young have to teach is how to let imagination and wonder open the doors to a life without the constriction of fear and limited thinking.

Step one is to stop looking back and start looking forward with joyous and eager anticipation of all that is yet to be learned enjoyed and experienced. That means you stop reporting endlessly on the fighting in the world - stop focusing on the ancient struggle - stop beating the drum of injustices and differences and inequalities. THAT IS THE OLD WAY AND IT will not usher in the new. THE NEW comes by turning entirely away from the old and invoking the new by focusing your full attention on it.

DAY 54 – REDEFINE YOURSELF

If you look up a word in the dictionary it will usually start out with the most commonly used words and definitions. If you look at a product in a store, the ingredient list will usually go in a descending order of what it contains the most of down to the least. And whether we like it or not, we all tend to label ourselves (though most of that comes from other people and the culture and we've accepted it somehow) - so if we looked at the back of you to read your label, what would it read? What would come at the top? If we looked you up in the dictionary, what would be the first words we'd find there?

You may find that you have accepted a lot of disempowering terms and self-concepts and put them way at the top. If that is the case, you may want to take some time to take back your power and REDEFINE YOURSELF in ways that empower you. YOU are in control here after all. You don't have to accept what the world or others have said or the category you've been slotted into. YOU get to choose now. Though it may be factual that you are divorced, disabled, unemployed, a senior, a recovering alcoholic or addict, a wounded veteran, dyslexic, overweight, shy, picky eater, pushy, an accountant, a survivor of something, the middle child, a spinster, an empty nester, or whatever, that does not mean that YOU need to lead with any of that or even have it on your list if you do not choose to put it there. Sometimes we don't even know we've drunk the cultural Kook-Aid and are going along with definitions that DISEMPOWER us and keep us down.

Ruminate for a while in the coming days to think about how YOU want to define yourself. <u>Who do YOU say that you are?</u> What do you want to lead with and accentuate? It doesn't matter if you could prove it in a court of law - we're being EMOTIONALLY BIASED with this exercise – meaning that we are deliberately making how we want to FEEL the top priority here. You may only doodle on paper napkins, but if you want to call yourself an artist, then you ARE an artist. You may only power walk 3 times a week but if you think of yourself as an athlete, then you ARE an athlete. We're not talking about putting on scrubs and doing surgery when you've never been to medical school! This is for YOU to begin to replace any old limiting thoughts about yourself with NEW IDEAS and concepts that lift you up rather than drag you down.

A lot of times our limiting concepts are used by us as an excuse to get out of doing things rather than just owning our "no thank you" - and perhaps that no longer serves you. It's something to consider. This isn't about trying to sound impressive to other people either, or wanting to control what someone else thinks about us. THIS IS FOR YOU to use to empower yourself if you've been thinking of yourself from a standpoint of limitation or loss or weaknesses rather than limitlessness and strength. Oh how I used to limit myself by retaining definitions put on me from DECADES gone by or from experts on talk shows and books or from doctors who were just taking their best guess, or from religions and spiritual philosophies and such - and they were almost always wrong, wrong, wrong - and very limiting or even shame-based.

If someone describes me as a spiritual stand up comic, I just walk away and avoid that person in the future. I reject that label because it diminishes me and what I do. I am changing people's lives. I'm not a clown or a comic and what I do is extremely important in the world. It's not entertainment, though people do find it entertaining. In my self-definition, funny isn't even in the top 10 ingredients, though I am very funny. I don't let others define me for myself. When others introduce me that way, I know they don't really get what I do or who I am so I don't take them seriously. I know they only see what's on the surface. Good for them. That has nothing to do with me. What they say or think about me is none of my business because it's just their projection. I cannot control what they say or think, but I can avoid them in the future and spend time with those who I resonate with. I define me and you define you. That is our unalienable right.

You can redefine FOR YOURSELF who and what you are, what you believe, what your life is about and for - you can further dissolve old lessons that are no longer true for you or that are holding you back. You can redefine what you believe success and wealth and love and peace and joy and EVERYTHING is to you - and you can keep doing it over and over again as you change and grow through this life. YOU get to choose. <u>You're the author of your story</u>.

Day 55 – Inquire Within

Amazing things happen when you begin to listen to the wisdom within you. There is no one way to seek it but many find it most easy to listen when in nature. You will find it if you seek it with diligence and patience - and trust.

No one else has your answers though others can help guide you to your own knowing. There is no expert on you but you. Your path and journey is unique to you. The Voice within you is your connection to Infinity Itself. You can trust it. <u>This Voice would never lead you to do any physical harm to another person or to yourself. It knows only love and peace.</u> Too much static from the outer world will tend to drown it out, so make some time every day to simply let all the thoughts slow down as you relax and breathe, relax and breathe. It makes no difference if you are sitting, lying down, walking, or running on the beach. Position is meaningless - openness is everything. You may even be dancing or singing in some instances. What is most important is the willingness and the inquiry.

The inquiry can be something as simple as saying to the Infinite Presence within, *"Speak Great Spirit (or Lord, or Goddess, or Father, or whatever name you prefer), I'm listening."* Continue to relax and breathe. Don't try. Let go of effort. Do not try hard - try soft. There should be no strain in this at all. If you experience strain, relax and go on with your day. You can come back to it again later if you like, but really, you may not need to. Once you've opened yourself up, you may find that your guidance and answers come from all kinds of people and circumstances that arise in the day - even in your dreams at night. It is a message of love and joy and peace and grace.

As you learn to trust your own inner voice, it becomes harder for you to fall into old habits of self-criticism and attack. There is infinite love and wisdom within you. Consult it often.

DAY 56 – INVOKE YOUR LIGHT BY FOCUSING ON IT

The world can be a very violent place. This is the way it's always been. It's not getting worse. It's not escalating. Cain killed Abel. Only 4 people on the planet, and two of them could not get along. The main difference now is not about the weapons and ways of doing harm, it's that we have immediate access to anything horrific or dark that is happening anywhere on the planet. And people are DRAWN to the darkness more than the Light. *"The Light came into the world, and men preferred darkness"* is true as ever. I have "un-friended" hundreds of people on social media who post nothing but whatever amplifies sadness, or injustice in the world. They speak of love, but actually are attracted to anything sad or dark - anything that makes them feel more disconnected from their Source.

People are violent for just one reason - they believe their stressful thoughts and then act on them. And since religion creates a lot of stressful thinking, religion is often right in the middle of the story. But religion is not the CAUSE of any of it - the cause is the same everywhere - it is the mind. It seems like the fighting in the world is about religion, or land, or retaliation, or poverty, or whatever - but it is really about the stressful thinking that is being believed and acted on.

The solution is to question our stressful thoughts and then turn them around to thoughts of peace, love and joy. How do we do that? Well, I've written six books that are full of HOW to do that, but rather than reaching for those books most people pull up a chair in front of the TV to watch more endless in-depth reporting on how fucked the world is and how in danger they may be. They post sad things on the Internet to show solidarity with the suffering that they do NOT show for those people when they are experiencing a win. Humans prefer the underdog and the suffering. It's where the attention goes and so we are actually teaching people that it's better to suffer than to thrive. If you thrive, you stand alone. If you are happy, there is something weird about you. You are not to be trusted. You don't "get it." Life is upside down and inside out. The great spiritual Masters have always taught that if you want to become peaceful and wise, go the road of the paradox. Everything in the physical is the opposite of Truth. To thrive here, you want to start to live in what I call "Opposite World" - the first shall be last, and the last shall be first.

We are in control of what we are putting in our Consciousness, in our mind, in our energetic field. And whatever we put there will have an effect on us - and then we'll wonder if we have a chemical imbalance that's making us depressed, or if we have a food allergy, or if it's the toxins various household products, or if it's hereditary. It's the THINKING that's hereditary. It's the THINKING that is causing most symptoms of un-wellness. All real healing is a shift in thinking and perception, whether there is a physical change or not.

The preamble to every message from God is, *"fear not, be not afraid."* Stop terrifying yourself. Stop being so tolerant of your own mind wandering and begin to FOCUS with determination on that which you choose to activate and amplify. Turn UP your Light instead of wringing your hands in worry, sadness and frustration. Stop beseeching a mythical deity in the sky to intervene and fix things. There is no such God and while masses pray to this Santa God, the wars rage on, children starve, people are tortured and abused and nothing changes. God is the Principle INSIDE every living creature - and It is activated by turning away from the darkness and amplifying the Light. *"Resist not evil"* the Master taught, because what we resist and fear, we are actually amplifying and creating more of through the creative agency of our own powerful minds. Stop thinking about what you don't want and cannot control and get back to focusing on INVOKING your inner Light and bringing it forth in all that you do, think, or say. The kingdom of Heaven is within you, bring it forth and soon you will see more and more evidence of it everywhere and in everything.

DAY 57 – PLEASE YOURSELF FIRST

Yes, you will need to please your employer or customers in certain ways in order to keep your agreements. And obviously in our relationships we WANT to please the other people because it feels good to bring joy to those we love. But you know that's not what I'm talking about.

This is about when we may try to please others by changing who we are in ways that we are doing only to get their approval and not because we are guided from within to make some positive change. Who you are is enough. Do your best and please yourself. There will always be someone to compare yourself to who may be "doing it better" than you are - or maybe they aren't doing it any better but for some reason they get a lot of glory and attention. Forget it. Keep your eyes on your own paper and do your life the way that pleases YOU even if no one notices or acknowledges it. YOU should acknowledge it every night when you put your head on the pillow. Thank yourself for doing such a good job - for showing up, prepared, on time, doing what you said you would do, with a good attitude. If you please yourself you will sleep much more soundly than if you are forever tap dancing and changing yourself all the time to get someone else to notice you and pat you on the back.

Live YOUR life. Do you. Your people will find you through vibrational matching, not through auditioning as a watered down self.

DAY 58 – COMPASSION IS OVER-RATED

The religious/spiritual types endlessly extol how important compassion is, but I have found compassion to be another one of those religious ideas that justify making yourself feel bad or projecting onto others that they should feel bad. Mostly compassion takes the place of something that IS important but more joyful - kindness and generosity.

Compassion is a FEELING - and usually not one that feels very good. It basically says, *"I FEEL BAD FOR YOU"* as if it is a gift to that person. Really, it does nothing to help anyone or anything. It is just a FEELING of *"my heart goes out to you"* - which is useless. Joining someone in their suffering just increases the vibration of suffering on the planet. ACTION helps. HELPING helps. FEELING bad for another person does nothing for that person or for you. KINDNESS is an ACTION. It is a doing. GENEROSITY IS AN ACTION. And remember, around here LOVE IS AN ACTION, not merely a feeling.

Compassion is often used to manipulate and I don't need to be manipulated thank you very much. I am a spiritually mature person who is able to make my own decisions. I don't need to see a commercial with sad music in the background of photos of abused animals in order to make a donation. I don't need to see starving children with flies all over them. I give and turn the channel when those commercials come on because they are TRYING to make me feel bad. I don't know about you, but when I feel bad I am more likely to NOT give - to just sit there feeling bad and hopeless, but compassionate. And I can pat myself on the back for being such a spiritual sensitive person who cares about the world, while I eat more chocolate cake to soothe MYSELF while doing NOTHING to actually help the one who is truly hurting.

When we replace compassion with kindness and generosity we are also eliminating an enormous amount of anger from our vibration because <u>the flip side of all that compassion is anger</u>. It's not just that we feel bad for the person suffering, we usually also have "righteous anger" at whoever or whatever we believe caused the suffering, whether it is a person, a society, a corporation, a political group, terrorists or whatever. Then we've got TWO BAD FEELINGS activated within our vibration!

I don't have to feel ANYTHING in order to give a blanket or sandwich to the homeless woman in the park. In fact, the people who are the most active in helping professions cannot afford to get their emotions activated with compassion endlessly or their adrenals would burn out so fast they'd barely be able to function. They are BUSY DOING the work of helping while maintaining an attitude of KINDNESS and GENEROSITY OF SPIRIT. There are plenty of people who FEEL BAD, feel compassion for the suffering, without ever lifting a finger to DO one single thing about it. Again, when we are run by our feelings and moods, our lives tend to be pretty messed up. I don't have to FEEL MOTIVATED to go to the gym and workout - all I need to do is GO and workout and I will have the RESULTS of the ACTION taken. And this is not about becoming an android with no feelings - quite the opposite in fact. It's about learning how to ACTIVATE what feels good in us under any and all circumstances. It's graduate Master's degree level spirituality.

This is another RADICAL "Opposite World" step forward to LIVING DELIBERATELY AND BY CHOICE rather than by the sentimental hypnotism of the culture in which "same old same old" is the norm. In fact, it FEELS GOOD to help when we are doing it because we want to. Helping others because we choose to can be another radical act of self-love because it makes US FEEL SO GOOD.

DAY 59 – NOT NUMERICAL, VIBRATIONAL

One of the first things we are taught as small children is to count - and it seems like we never stop counting. The world is endlessly taking score of this and that. Numbers have the odds against us most of the time. It took me a long time to realize how stressful this can be and how little it actually has to do with reality. We're counting the dollars in the bank, the chronological age of the body, the number on the scales, the temperature outside - and we make ridiculous assumptions based on numbers. The numbers are always too low or too high it seems - too young to drive, too short to get on this roller coaster, too old to start a family, too heavy to wear that, too light to play that sport, and then eventually too old to drive. Numbers have a tendency to speak of limitation and seeming impossibilities in so many ways.

I live in a place where I see a lot of couples that have a huge disparity in their chronological ages and yet they seem very happy and in love. They are matched VIBRATIONALLY rather than generationally. We are taught these kinds of relationships never work out - though most of these couples have been together a very long time. I guess they didn't read the report on how this isn't cool and shouldn't work. The world is full of experts on odds and how things are not likely to work out. The same with long-distance relationships - too many miles between and everyone knows they NEVER work out - except for the people who live outside the cultural norms and decide to make up the life THEY choose.

I've lived very abundantly at times when the number of dollars coming in was not that high, and lived in a lot of fear at times when the number was much higher. I discovered that wealth and prosperity is vibrational more than numerical. There were times when I felt very good . . . until I got on the scales and saw the number. Then, I allowed THAT to change my vibration! We are inundated with so much data that is supposed to mean something when really it means very little when we are tuned into the Broader Perspective of the Universal Flow.

We are fed a steady diet of information in this world, and very little of it is neutral. It's mostly skewed and MEANT to sway us one way or another. Most frequently it is meant to manipulate us into buying or buying into something. You are a mystic. You have much more profound ways of knowing and understanding than through numbers and data. Do not trust your eyes alone, they will deceive you.

If you want more peace, clarity and joy in your life, start thinking more in terms of VIBRATION. What's the VIBE of this relationship, this job, your health, this food, your finances, and everything else? TUNE IN to the vibrations in the way that Yoda told Luke to feel the Force. Stop limiting yourself according to the skewed information the culture is endlessly throwing at us. Things have never been better in this world but there are more 24 hour news channels than ever and they NEED to have content and they NEED ratings, so they sensationalize everything in an effort to scare you into watching and into buying things that you think will keep you safe or make you more desirable and lovable. TUNE THAT SHIT OUT and tune into the Universal

Broader Perspective of your gut intuition - not your heart, your heart will usually lead you down the sentimental wrong road. The heart and mind are a fabulous team members but a horrible leaders. Consult your heart and mind, but let your gut make the final decisions and guide you as you tune into the Force from which all Life flows.

DAY 60 – USE YOUR VOICE

In the beginning was the Word. In the Judeo-Christian Bible, God SPOKE the world into existence. That is how important the voice is. That is how important it is to speak our own truth - even if no one listens or hears. We find our voice by using it with conviction. People who love themselves speak up and believe they are worth being heard.

It's not about shouting. Shouting often makes it more difficult for others to hear you anyhow. If we keep on using our voice, with courage and conviction, over time there are people who will hear. There are things that you need to say. And the more you speak your love, the better you'll feel eventually.

Yes, some people will misunderstand you. You may stammer or babble or your voice may quiver. It's okay. You'll get clearer the more you speak. You deserve to be heard. You're important. Your words matter. No need to MAKE anyone listen either. The more you speak up, the more you'll attract people on your frequency who are ready and wanting to hear what you have to say.

As a child I was taken to speech therapists and I was made fun of and tormented because of my voice until I was well into my 20's. But I also kept being picked to do things that required that I speak in public. It terrified and thrilled me at the same time. I had to keep walking through my fear and resistance in order to achieve my dreams and goals. Now I've spent the past 25 years speaking for a living and it still gets me into lots of trouble. So what? You've got to use your voice if you want to be fully alive. It may not be spoken - it may be written, or sung, or painted, or danced, or crafted, or thousands of other expressions of your voice - these are all ways to speak your truth, to speak your world into existence. There is no one way. Find yours and speak up.

DAY 61 – THREE THINGS

Here is a daily exercise to do which can help you in immeasurable ways if you remember to commit to it and keep it up. <u>Every night when you climb into bed, gently go over your day and find 3 things that you can be grateful to yourself for, honor yourself for, or appreciate about yourself.</u> Make it up any way that FEELS GOOD to YOU.

So mix it up any way you like - it can be things that you did or accomplished that day or qualities about yourself that you like or progress that you made or whatever it is that is you giving you a nice soothing pat on the back as you go to sleep.

Far too many people spend that time after climbing into bed to go over what went wrong, blame themselves and others, remember how they blew it, worry about tomorrow and so on. That is SELF-TORTURE. The way we replace a bad habit is to replace it with a positive one. And "Three Things" is the start of a positive new bed time habit that will help you sleep like a baby.

And remember, ALL the boot camp exercises are OPTIONAL and are meant to make you FEEL GOOD. If an exercise is stressful and not fun, it's not for you and you should skip it. It's YOUR boot camp and YOU are the author of your self-love journey. Make it work for you.

DAY 62 – NOT SPEND, INVEST

When you love yourself, quality becomes more important than quantity. When you think of yourself and your life as important, you begin to think less of how you "spend" your day and think more in terms of how you invest your time, energy and resources. It's a shift in Consciousness more than anything else.

You may do many of the same things, but you begin to think of them differently. It's not so much that we do different things as that we do things differently. You're not "wasting the day" by staying inside and reading or taking a nap, you're investing in your self-care. You're not being frivolous by getting a massage, but are investing in your mental and physical health and well being.

If you haven't already made this shift, begin to think about it now and how something so subtle can be so enormously powerful. The message here is INVEST IN YOURSELF. Personal growth and renewal is often the very last thing on people's list of what is important and it's why Stephen Covey wrote so powerfully on "keep first things first." If we are not taking care of ourselves and our own personal growth by investing in our continual learning and expansion, we have less and less to draw on from our internal reserves. His habit of "sharpen the saw" is about taking care of the instrument of "self" through continual self-renewal in order to LIVE LIFE MORE FULLY AND ABUNDANTLY.

"Sharpen the saw," means that instead of sawing harder and faster because our saw is so rusty and we're in a hurry, we TAKE THE TIME to stop sawing while we sharpen our instrument. Then, when we return to sawing, we make quick progress with much less struggle and effort.

So, how are you investing in yourself?

Day 63 – Turn It Around

One of the ways we can torment ourselves endlessly is through negative assumptions. It pays to start to become VERY aware of what you are assuming about people, life and situations. What we assume can either lift us up or hurl us into the ditch. What we assume, we are ACTIVATING and attracting to us.

A friend of mine has an office management job and a part of it that she really did not like was collections. She would have to call various clients who were behind in their payments to try to get them to pay. She is an extremely kind person and gets along with everyone, but this kind of seemingly confrontational work was difficult for her. What made it REALLY difficult was her assumption that they didn't really want to pay. It turned them into adversaries that she would then feel in opposition to - the sense that she needed to DO SOMETHING that would MAKE THEM PAY while still remaining calm and keeping the business relationship intact. Very stressful.

We do this a lot in life. We have various partnerships that we begin to make mental adversarial assumptions about and it torments us with stress, worry, grievances, frustration, and manipulation - messy stuff. Or we assume they won't hire us, date us, tell us the truth, keep their word, be on time, forgive us, listen, give us the promotion, and so on. We assume something is going to be hard before we've even taken the first step. Some of us make lots of negative assumptions and we believe we are right without ever questioning the theory. We go in with our dukes us and then wonder why things go so poorly and why we feel so exhausted and frustrated.

I told my friend to "turn it all around" and begin to THINK of these clients differently. <u>She needed to ASSUME THEY WANT TO PAY</u> and that they <u>will</u> pay. She is only calling as a friendly reminder or to find out if there's anything she can do to help with different arrangements, etc. She had to see them all as on the same side and think kindly of them instead of as people she was trying to force to do something. She had to see them as THRIVING AND ABUNDANT rather than as people who have money problems or who are resistant to paying. It meant flipping the whole story and coming at it from the opposite direction. It was all about Consciousness, Consciousness, Consciousness.

So, she tried it. And . . . it worked. Her resistance evaporated as she started seeing them differently and in response they shifted and started to pay their bills. In fact, now other companies call her for her expertise on how she does so well with collections - the very thing that she hated about her job. She turned it around and released herself from a tremendous amount of stress and resistance.

Start paying attention and noticing when you are mentally bracing yourself for something because you've already made a negative assumption - then, do yourself a favor and turn it around.

DAY 64 – "I LOVE MYSELF, THEREFORE . . . "

Again, let me remind you that you already DO and always have loved yourself. It is natural and you were born that way. It is already there underneath various layers of programming. Therefore, we are not TRYING to love ourselves but merely dissolving any thoughts of shame, guilt and unworthiness that have built up over the years, and that's what this boot camp has been doing all along. So be sure you are NOT going around thinking or saying "I don't love myself" - because that is LIE and a terrible affirmation.

Instead, begin practicing saying to yourself, *"I love myself, therefore* _____ *"* and fill in the blanks as you go along. You will begin to find that there is all kinds of evidence of how much you DO love yourself already. There are some very bare minimum things I will assume about you to help you prime the pump (but I know there are much larger things than this that you can begin to recognize and say or write down).

You love yourself therefore:

- You've made sure you have a home to live in.
- You've made sure you have a bed to sleep in.
- You've allowed yourself use of a computer to read this.
- You fed yourself today.
- You've gone out and chosen clothes that you like so that you can wear them.
- You probably bathed and brushed your teeth and groomed yourself today.

- You maintain some personal relationships.
- You read books to uplift and encourage yourself.

You get the idea. Practice looking at your life this way and using this statement to show how much you actually ARE taking care of yourself, remembering that love is an ACTION, not merely the ephemeral *feeling* of affection. <u>Make a habit of looking around your life and recognize that YOU CREATED THIS LIFE through your Consciousness and actions - a home, food, relationships, reminders of good times such as photos or mementos, pets, work, and on and on.</u> Make it a habit to gather up evidence of how much you already love and care for yourself - that it is not something you will achieve later on. YOU ALREADY LOVE YOURSELF. We are not taking something on; we're taking something off. We're taking off any lies that we've taken on over the course of living.

DAY 65 – FOCUS ON THE LOVE

It's a tremendous waste of time and energy, not to mention cruel, to focus on the love that was not given to us in the past or that is not being given by someone now when there are always people around who DO love us.

Perhaps we were not given approval by family or loved ones or a mate in the past - and we allowed that to program some erroneous thoughts about our own worthiness. Those beliefs will only color our experience of the present the way a piece of dirt on a projector lens would project onto a movie screen and blot out some wonderful character or scene.

Instead of focusing on the best friend who loves and approves of us the way we are, we chew on the disapproval of someone we barely know or who is long gone from our lives. We may even be focusing on trying to earn the approval or affection of one person, while ignoring the friends who are here now giving us support, kindness and affection.

It can take some practice to actually NOTICE love and approval when you've inadvertently trained yourself to notice hurt, pain and judgment. You may not even realize that you push people away with negative talking and attitudes. It is an adjustment to go from gathering up evidence of lack of love to gathering up evidence of love and approval but with practice it gets easier and easier.

One sure sign that our self-love is coming forth is when we have less and less interest in those whom it doesn't feel good to spend time with. Instead we are drawn more and more to relationships in which after we've been together, whether for coffee or lunch or working on a project, we leave the encounter feeling uplifted and good instead of insecure, worried and guilty. Love FEELS GOOD.

DAY 66 – YOUR SCARS ARE BEAUTIFUL

The things you feel embarrassed by or that you try to hide . . . well, they *may* be what is most lovable about you to some. They may be your path into the hearts of others. Your greatest failures may be exactly where you are ultimately most able to help others. Most everyone is scarred in one way or another.

Bring it all out into the light. You are beautiful - all of you. So much energy is wasted in shame and embarrassment and in trying to be something different. You're still here so there must be some awesome reason why the world needed you - scars and wounds and all, whether they are physical or emotional. It may have something to do with inspiring the rest of us so please don't hide.

DAY 67 – GO WITH THE FLOW

I have loved this saying, and I have hated it. But that was all before I really understood it and I think that most people don't really see the whole picture of it, even the people who love and use it the most. Now that I really get it, I love it and I love to go with the flow.

The misunderstanding is about "the flow" - as if it's a "thing out there" apart from us that has volition and asserts itself onto us. It's as if we're just being swept along for the ride and all we can do is try to keep our heads above water, swim or if we're one of the "lucky" ones, ride or surf on it like a pro to the sunny shores. Some say that the river just goes where it goes and you cannot change it. Some people are on a good river and some are not - nothing you can do about it but make the best of the one you're on. This is nonsense.

The Truth is, we <u>are</u> the flow and the flow is us. The flow is an aspect of Universal Mind responding and moving in response to our thoughts, moods, attitudes, actions, perceptions - basically, in response to our CONSCIOUSNESS. <u>When we change our Consciousness, the flow changes in response to us. Our Consciousness actually SUMMONS the flow!</u> Therefore, it's useless and hopeless to fight the flow. The smartest most efficient thing to do is to always GO WITH THE FLOW since we are the one who summoned it to begin with. But if we do not like the way it's flowing, then we have to change our Consciousness - and when we do that, the flow itself changes.

There is nothing denied us as long as it doesn't interfere with the free will of another. Life is open to us and we can live the life we choose. We don't have to EARN it or struggle for it. The good stuff doesn't go to the brightest or most talented or beautiful or most deserving. It goes to the ones who are lined up with the good stuff in Consciousness. Therefore there's no reason to EVER get down on yourself or feel that anything is too good for you or that if you just struggle and strive against the flow enough you'll get there. Instead, relax MORE and remember to BE ON YOUR OWN TEAM. When you are on your own team it's much easier to affect the flow in positive joyful ways.

Keep in mind always, your own self-concept will affect the flow more than any action you could ever take in the world. It's not about controlling the flow, it's about influencing. Control will just make you more rigid and tense, which fucks up your flow. <u>Relax. The flow is your friend</u>. Talk to it, work with it, have fun with it - and go with it on the most magnificent ride you can imagine.

DAY 68 – THE RIGHT DIRECTION

Most of our progress in this program is invisible on a day-to-day basis. Particularly with our boot camp we may find that everything externally appears exactly as it was on day one. Some may have lost weight, cleaned out the garage, or done any number of other physical things . . . but it is ultimately our THINKING that we are changing and that may not be very obvious to other people for a while.

But, by now you have most likely FELT many shifts within you. Ernest Holmes was so wonderful about reminding us that as long as we are making tiny inroads to feeling even a little more peaceful, a tiny bit more expectant of good, a bit less guilty or tormented, WE ARE GOING IN THE RIGHT DIRECTION. I think of it as effort without struggle. It even takes effort to change the TV channel using the remote control, so we often erroneously use the word "effortless" when we really mean "struggleless."

It takes effort to make new choices, to think new thoughts, to undo old programming and to dissolve old paradigms. It takes consistency, forgiveness when we are not consistent (because, duh), commitment, and WILLINGNESS to keep going forward - to not give up on ourselves. We tend to dwell too much on the failures of yesterday instead of simply using them as the learning curve for doing better today. Let's not do that. Dwell on the good as much as possible.

As always, it's progress, not perfection.

DAY 69 – VALUE YOUR TALENTS

A lot of folks love to "talk" about gratitude in the same way they like to talk about love, as if it's a "FEELING" and not what it really is, an ACTION. Feelings are ephemeral and cannot be counted on. They rise and fall and come and go. True gratitude is more than a feeling or a mood. It's amazing how many talk endlessly about gratitude without ever actually saying "thank you." So many think that prosperity is about getting and receiving rather than generating and producing. All this focus on getting leaves those they get from feeling depleted and used. It's a terrible thing to keep your talents and gifts locked up without ever sharing them with others, but it's just as terrible to share them where they are taken for granted by those who have entitlement issues.

So, <u>be very careful whom you are sharing your talents and gifts with</u>. Be certain that YOU are honoring your gift, because they may not. And if you have problems with self-love, you may actually be trying to earn or buy their affection, which is a losing game. And YOU are the one hurting yourself. It's not them. They are just doing their thing while you keep giving, giving, giving to people and places that will never bear good fruit.

<u>When you value yourself, you value your talents and gifts. When you value your talents, you give them where they can do the most good and where they are the most appreciated.</u> Just a quick "fyi" - the kid in the story "The Giving Tree" was a whiny little creep and the tree was an enabler who allowed the kid to never have to experience what

a mature love is really all about. That relationship was fucked up.

Your talents are sacred and precious. Don't cast your pearls before the savages. Honor your gifts and give them where they are understood and valued so that both giver and receiver are truly blessed. Those who are truly grateful are saying "Thank you" many many times every day, not just on holidays and special occasions.

DAY 70 – FUCK THE CRITICS

As human beings, we like to see what others are doing and weigh in with our opinion as if the media were waiting for a press release from us. I do it quite frequently, but less and less as I release it as a bad habit. *"Cease to cherish opinions"* the sage reminds us. Cherishing our opinions usually just causes us mental and emotional discomfort no matter how smug, superior or even well meaning we may feel about what we're saying.

I've been teaching for 30 years and in that time I've spoken to thousands and thousands of people. Additionally, I've written and published more than half a dozen books. And of course lots of people have had lots of opinions over the years on how I "coulda-shoulda-woulda" done it all differently, better, and more to their liking. The strongest and most negative opinions tend to come from those who've never spoken before a group in their lives and who've never so much as written an article for a newsletter. Everyone is an expert on what others are doing, have you noticed? And I admit, it's very difficult to not let it get to you when someone attacks something you've created or that you're doing, or just attacks you personally for who and what you are.

With the Internet it is very easy now to publicly attack so it's not just public people like myself who get it these days - the neighbors can start anonymously posting horrible gossip about your children, or criticize the way you are raising your kids. Perhaps it's done in person by family members during the holiday gatherings when they may feel free to go over all your fuckups from 20 years ago. We live in a world of opinions just waiting to be voiced.

Over time, you may start to withdraw from life and start wanting to play it safe so you won't be criticized anymore. You may stop trying new things out of fear that it won't work and it'll be more fodder for the critics. Without meaning to, you may stop exploring and discovering - in other words you've let the opinions of others stop you from living and growing.

Fuck em. And I mean that in a very non-aggressive metaphorical way - not that you need to actually communicate that to them, because it may just make it worse. If you need to confront someone, it should be done after careful consideration and looking within to see if you really need to say something or not. You are probably a much sweeter person than I am so you might just want to say to yourself, *"Well, that's their opinion but it has nothing to do with me."* The point is to keep living your life to please yourself, considering only those close to you who are directly affected and leaving everyone else out of your happiness equation. Most of the time they are just blindly yapping and don't even know you're taking it to heart. Or they are just trying to get a rise out of you. Always consider the source. Often it is coming from someone who is already very insecure about their own failures and they are simply projecting.

Keep evolving and expanding no matter how much they talk. Go within and follow your own inner wisdom and guidance. I still fail almost every day, and frequently it is in public. So what? Keep going and enjoying your life right up to the very last day on the planet. The purpose of life is joyful expansion, remember?

DAY 71 – SURRENDER TO GRACE

One of the most radical acts of self-love is the surrender to Grace. It is an act of self-love because it relieves you of the overwhelming burden of endless pushing, resistance and struggle. By surrendering to Grace we give deep rest and sustenance to our entire Team - body, mind, spirit and heart.

Grace is the unmerited favor of the Universe. It cannot be earned or it would not be Grace, it would be payment. Grace does not come to us; it is ever present but unnoticed by the mind that is relentlessly racing from thing to thing to thing, with exhaustive plans and schemes. Plans are very good when they arise from a mind that is open and relaxed. This is what Grace gives us.

HOW do we surrender to Grace? Simple, just STOP right now, right where you are. STOP for even just an instant and let your shoulders, neck and jaw relax as you take a deep breath. Now, mentally wave a white flag as you tell the Universe, the Force, the Great Mother, *"I surrender to Your infinite Love and Grace now. Bring my good here to me now, or guide me to the open doors. I am ready to let my life work in the most wonderful and unexpected ways. I look forward to watching how it all unfolds. I'm listening - lead me on."*

DAY 72 – BE UNCONDITIONAL

We are far enough along in boot camp now to introduce this. It's graduate level stuff because for some of you it will be a TREMENDOUS PUSH. It's practicing unconditional love as an ACTION. What that means is that your love for yourself not be conditional. Self-love must not be doled out because you've performed perfectly today, nor is it to be withdrawn because you've messed up. It must be love that is not based on conditions - loving yourself when you are doing fabulously <u>and</u> when you are a mess, when you are all dressed up and when you are sick and look like hell, when you ace the exam and when you've failed for the 20th time. Un-con-dit-ion-al. Period.

And it's graduate level when it comes to actions because that's where folks have the hardest time - SHOWING UP FOR THEMSELVES NO MATTER WHAT. Remember, it's like a mother caring for a baby - it's not about FEELING LIKE showing up for yourself, because many times you will NOT "feel like it." This is where we betray ourselves and where it shows through. We may SAY we love ourselves but then when we take a look at our ACTIONS we may see that in fact we've abandoned ourselves and are not treating ourselves with respect, care, diligence - sometimes not even with the same effort that we put into taking care of a pet. Imagine if you loved yourself as unconditionally as your dog loves you, or even as much as you love your dog.

So, this is a biggie and now that we are almost in the home stretch of boot camp it's time to really go for it. Just observe for a while to notice if you may have unconsciously set conditions on your self-love. One way you can notice is how much you beat yourself up when you make a mistake or when things go wrong - and then what you DO in the aftermath, particularly in terms of not showing up for yourself or making it an excuse to backslide instead of just forgiving yourself, learning from it and moving on.

DAY 73 – YOU

You are a unique individual. There is no one like you. What difference then can it make what others are being, doing, having, achieving or experiencing? You are no carbon copy. You didn't come here to fall in line and produce more sameness or to compare yourself to the status quo. We live in times in which we know far too much about far too many people - from "reality" TV to all the forms of social media, to everything in between we see what others are putting out there. It's mostly just meaningless data that is wildly skewed or outright false.

Here and now, right where you are, is what matters. If you had nothing to compare your NOW with, how would it feel to you? This home, this body, this face, these clothes, this work, this health, this life, these relationships, this solitude or crowd, this great activity or quiet, this heat or cold, clear or cloudy - how would it FEEL to you if you had nothing and no one to compare it with at all?

In fact, if you had no one ever telling you how you "should" or "shouldn't" be or have been, wouldn't there be no self-criticism to work on dissolving to begin with? If there were no "experts" around to tell you how to live, what to eat, how to exercise, what the latest thing is, what qualifies as art, what the "good life" looks like, what you need to do or have financially, what the future might hold - if all of that did not exist and you had only yourself to rely on to guide you as to how to feel every day, how might you feel?

What I'm suggesting of course is that we have many voices in our head that are drowning out our own true inner-voice. We came here to create our own life from out of the vast Creative Agency of Source and then are methodically trained out of all original thought or any behavior that does not align with the "norm" of our culture. Fuck that shit. YOU are more than an imitator. You are an original. Shut that noise down more and turn within to find your way. Maybe the things you've been working so hard to change are just fine the way they are.

DAY 74 – GO YOUR OWN WAY

I tend to wear women's jewelry - rings, bracelets and ear posts. I like it. It brings me joy. And even in the "gay community" (there really is no such thing), there is quite a lot of disdain and judgment for anything not "masculine." So what? Again, fitting in is for sponges, not people. And self-love is very difficult if you are not even expressing yourself in the way that brings you the most joy.

If you want to keep up a Christmas tree all year long, good for you. If you like to keep a spare room full of neatly organized classic Barbie dolls in glass cabinets, eat breakfast foods for dinner every night, paint or draw for 10 hours at a stretch, go to science fiction or comic book conventions, travel endlessly, never go anywhere, live in a tiny house, do naked yoga, shave your head or grow your hair down to your ankles, or anything else that brings you joy - well, as long as it's not hurting you or another - if it's not an obsession that torments you and puts your health, sanity or finances at risk, go for it.

Of course, you may have to dress a certain way for your job, or if you have a mate and children or roommates then you have to negotiate shared living spaces and other aspects of how you live, but again, if it's not hurting you or the family and the only objection is that you are weird, I say be weird and enjoy your abnormal journey. It's not really up to others to "get you" or approve of your choices. If it is harming you or holding you back from experiencing things that you WANT to experience, then I would say it is probably not an expression of true self-love and you may actually be doing it as a way to keep people away. Only your own inner investigation can reveal this to you.

If you are even reading this, there is a very good chance that you are the weird one in your family or group. Good for you. Rock it. Luckily we live in times when us weirdos can find each other quite easily across time and space through the fabulous Internet and such. There's a tribe out there somewhere for you if you want one. And if you don't, that's cool too.

DAY 75 – CONSIDER THE LILIES

It's wonderful to be engaged in creating, doing, and having busy hands and an active mind when our lives are balanced. Most everyone likes to have something to look forward to DOING most days whether it is work or play or anything else that stimulates or engages us.

The problem is how much we tend to allow STRUGGLE and resistance to enter the picture as if it were just part of life and completely inevitable. It's not even that we may do it in our jobs; we may do it in many different ways in order to JUSTIFY OUR VERY EXISTENCE ON THE EARTH. We act as if we have to earn our oxygen every day in this Western world. It's not like this everywhere. It's cultural in various places and you know if you are a part of one of these cultures.

Did you know that is it not POSSIBLE to waste a day simply because you didn't "accomplish" something? However, I would agree that we often waste a lot of our lives in needless and fruitless worrying and guilt over nothing. You are worthy because you exist - period. If you breathe in and out all day long, you are providing the planet with nitrogen and oxygen and carbon dioxide with every exhale. Good for you. We thank you. Good job. So, let go of any foolish guilt you may have over what did or did not get "accomplished" this week and realize there is a time and a season for everything. Sometimes busy, sometimes not. Sometimes sowing, sometimes reaping, sometimes summer and sometimes winter.

Jesus said a few thousand years ago to consider the lilies of the field - they are never afraid of not accomplishing anything or earning their place in the world and yet they are provided for without struggle or suffering. So are we when we let go of worry and relax into the Flow of Life from which all sustenance is drawn.

DAY 76 – ROMANCE YOURSELF

What most of us think of when it comes to romance is really just setting a mood, an atmosphere, and an ambiance that encourages intimacy. It's a way to slow down through attention to detail. It's another ACT of love and it is very individual though you really cannot do it with a cell phone in your hand.

It's about slowing down to the speed of love - putting away the phone and doing something that allows you to take your time to really appreciate and savor the environment. And for many people it takes EFFORT to slooooooow down this much.

It makes no difference if it's taking a walk in nature with yourself, or going to a quiet cozy place for coffee or lunch, or snuggling up on the sofa with a good book, or lighting candles as you step into a luxurious bubble bath, or getting a massage or pedicure, a long drive along the coast or up into the mountains, an afternoon matinee at the movies, or simply sit outside and watch the sun set - it's whatever FEELS like you giving yourself loving beautiful attention where you leave behind the rush-rush of the mind and get into marinating in FEELINGS of luxuriating in the now.

Remember, the Universe is RESPONDING to us like a mirror and will reflect back to us the thoughts we have about ourselves and the kind of care we take OF this fabulous self. Treat yourself today or very very soon to a little romance.

DAY 77 – REMEMBER THE TIMES

Think back to the times that you have brought joy to others, to anyone. Remember when you've made a friend smile, or a baby laugh, or a dog wag it's tail. Reflect and ruminate on when you've helped anyone, cheered someone up, made life brighter. Think of the times when it was so clear that they felt what you were giving and bringing. Think of the look on their face - a look of joy, or appreciation, or comfort. Realize you have the power to soothe and uplift.

If you really do this, if you take the time to sit with it and truly FEEL it, you will feel an increase in appreciation and love for yourself. You will see the power of it and it will humble and strengthen you at the same time. It will feed your soul and you may even cherish yourself a little bit more. It's one of the wonders of this life.

DAY 78 – SEEK OUT THE GOOD NEWS

There was a time when TV news was only aired several times a day. There were morning news shows, the 6:00 evening news and then the 11:00 news. But now we have 24/7 news networks, which are big business with sponsors and huge staffs to pay. It's a competitive business, which must get ratings to survive so they must constantly drive people to their TV channel and their online sites and social media. Unfortunately, the most surefire way to sell anything is through FEAR. Therefore, they are not really in the business of reporting anymore but rather the business of selling and pushing fear. Fear is HUGE BUSINESS in the western world. You could call us the "fear-eaters" because so many consume fear in mass quantities every day. It is an almost passive kind of self-hatred and attack on the mind. Again, it is being complicit in your own destruction.

It takes EFFORT and work to find the good news every day even though there is overwhelmingly more good news every day than bad news. Good news simply does not sell. A good deed will receive 2 social media hits compared to 100 million hits of the actions of one insane individual. Man's inhumanity to man is as old as Cane killing Abel, but it will still receive 99.99999% of the attention compared to man helping his neighbor.

So many people eat the daily POISON, and it IS poison, of the worldly bad news. Then they will regurgitate it, post about it online, bring it up at dinner parties, argue about it with family members that they would have otherwise gotten along with very well . . . all without realizing it is destroying their own immune system, dumping acid into their stomachs, raising the blood pressure, fucking up the chemical factory of the brain and causing them to not be able to sleep peacefully at night. They do not make the connection to taking in and activating enormous amounts of fear and their own sanity and inner peace. They go to family gatherings and start conversations about what they DISAGREE with others about instead of bring up where they DO agree. They stir up trouble and then wonder why their mind and heart feels so troubled.

It takes TREMENDOUS courage and will power to turn it off. The machine itself tells you that to turn it off is irresponsible. It hypnotizes people into thinking they NEED and are OBLIGATED to pay attention to all the pain and suffering in the world - that it is MORALLY RIGHT to poison yourself a little every day, that it's your rent for living on the planet. But that is all just the bullshit of the tormented that preaches the gospel of torment.

Self-love says, "repent." Repent means to turn around - you're going the wrong way. Turn away from the endless stream of bad news and begin to seek out the news that makes YOU FEEL GOOD. You have to love yourself enough to each day SEEK OUT THE GOOD NEWS THAT WILL LIFT YOU UP instead of eating the poison of the day.

DAY 79 – WALK THROUGH THE FEAR

The fact is, more people are stopped by fear than by any real obstacles. It may not look like fear - it may look like a "valid reason", or exhaustion, or lack of resources, or a million and one other things that come up. Do NOT let fear stop you no matter how it arises. YOU ARE WORTH THE EFFORT. Rest, regroup, renew - but do not give up on yourself.

And let go of time even if it's going to take 40 years - 40 years are going to pass anyhow so why not use them to INVEST in yourself and your dreams? It's only the fucked-up CULTURE that is age-obsessed. The Universe has NO IDEA how old or young you are. Begin to realize now that your excuses are just that, excuses. Instead of worrying about what other people will think about you or say about you, use that same time and energy to research people who have achieved their dreams in spite of their age, lack of resources and so on. CHOOSE TO SEEK INSPIRATION instead of justification for not trying.

The way to walk through fear is to build up your courage and inspiration by filling your heart and mind with the images of those who've gone before you, those who've gone beyond all the cultural stories and invested in their own dreams. And be aware, they were probably terrified at times too. Everyone faces fear and often on a daily basis. It's still no excuse for not going for the life you want. No one is stopping you but you and a ridiculous story of limitation playing in your mind. YOU define yourself. And though you may fall down 10,000 times along the way, so what? Take a nice long nap, and then get up and get back on the path again. I still face some measure of fear every day, but I've learned how to encourage and soothe myself into moving forward. Remember, progress, not perfection.

DAY 80 – YOU ARE A POWERFUL CREATOR

Now we are in the final stretch of boot camp. It's time to take a good hard look at yourself in the mirror and recognize the magnificent being that you are. There is no room anymore for being a beggar waiting to accept the crumbs that are given by others. You have the self-esteem, the courage, the chutzpah, the nerve, the Grace and the inner strength to go directly to Source for your infinite good.

You are no longer waiting for permission, nor for the world to take notice. You are about your Father-Mother's business of channeling LIFE through you into form in this world. You are coming close to graduation from boot camp and you have done very well indeed. Begin now to prepare for your graduation by thinking about those you will lovingly invite in Consciousness to attend, what you will wear, what the environment will be, how you will stand and hold yourself, what you will wear, and what you will have learned and mastered in these 90 days. Reflect, and then vision and use your DIVINE IMAGINATION to begin to create your future.

You are no longer a grunt; you are a Soldier of Light! Get ready to go out into the world and shine. This is your time. You are ready.

DAY 81 – MAKE PEACE WITH YOURSELF

One thing I emphasized at the start of this boot camp had to do with not rejecting aspects of ourselves - that we cannot really live in self-love if there are parts of ourselves that we disown or hate. On the other hand, many of us have aspects of our BEHAVIOR or personality or bodies or whatever that we may find hard to really love fully. These are often the parts that we've tried and tried to change but simply had little to no success in making any real change. In these cases, it's important to remember the law of Consciousness and energy that says, *"what you resist, persists."* What we go to war with in ourselves often just gets larger and more strengthened.

Therefore, it's often best to simply make peace with these aspects of ourselves. You don't have to LOVE every aspect of yourself in order to really live a life of self-love, but you cannot be at WAR with aspects of yourself. You may be extremely shy and you've tried everything to be more outgoing with no success - and you just cannot seem to LOVE that part of yourself either. You know intellectually that shyness is not a fault; you know that there is nothing wrong with it, you understand all the blah, blah, blah, but you still cannot really seem to LOVE that part of your personality. Okay, fine. Make peace with it then. Fighting it will just make you insane and more focused on this ONE part of you instead of beating the drum of all the things that you DO love about yourself. MAKE PEACE WITH IT and understand that the Universe is not held back by ANY aspect of you - it IS block by your ATTITUDE about any aspect of yourself though.

To make peace with yourself is a shift in your attitude about yourself. To make peace is to go from resistance to gentle acceptance. This is NOT about a depressing resignation, but it is also not about making fun of yourself with self-denigrating humor. It's a cheerful acceptance of MAKING PEACE as you might make peace with a beloved pet who has some aspects that you find less than adorable at times. In some cases, this is a much easier step to make than a full embracing. It's totally fine. Peace and acceptance is a HUGE step in loving ourselves.

DAY 82 – BURN THE BOXES

The world is more obsessed with boxes than ever. From the day you are born there are forms being filled out about you and YOU are checked off as a this or that. And as time marches on in the culture the forms just keep adding boxes so that no one will feel left out which is all well and good - I'm all for everyone feeling seen and included. The problem is that it also defines, isolates and separates us in so many ways.

But those boxes are only emblematic of all the other boxes we don't realize we've been put into and put ourselves into. Those boxes are the paradigms then of how we see our life and world, of what we think it acceptable for us, and it's usually something that we've been hypnotized into believing without ever really thinking about it and deciding for ourselves. The boxes are about our gender, our sexuality, our age, our race, our economic background, our education, where we live, where we "should" be at this point in our lives, and so much more.

I lived in a very tiny box inside a box inside a box inside a box for so many years and I had no idea how miserable it was making me. For a long time I lived in the box of what I thought a "spiritual teacher" was and how I needed to behave. That box left me nearly paralyzed with depression and I was ready to go get a job in a mall until I decided to simply discard that box and be who it was natural for me to be - to do it MY way. And that's when my career really took off. Yes, it pissed people off and still does at times, but that is not my problem. That is THEIR box, not mine.

What many outsiders may call your "reinvention" is usually nothing more than you burning an old box that no longer fits so that you can stretch out and become more of what you already were underneath all along. It's not reinvention, it's recognition.

Day 83 – Share Your Love and Appreciation

By now your self-love is probably soaring at times. This is the perfect time to introduce a Principle that will not only keep this momentum going, but amp it up considerably. It can actually become so enjoyable that for some it has become a "magnificent obsession" in their lives.

Here it is - <u>give what you want</u>. Since thoughts do not leave their source, what you think about others never leaves your own Consciousness and it wallpapers the walls of your mind. If you think kindly of others and appreciate something about them, you will FEEL the result of that approval too! And if you want to triple or quadruple the effects, <u>EXPRESS your love and approval to others with the same kind of frequency, detail and enthusiasm that you would want others to express it to you</u>. It will go out to them, but it will also STAY WITH YOU. Whether they truly receive it or not is none of your business. Your part is merely to give it out, and as you practice it more and more without attachment to an outcome, you will be drawn to those who willingly and gratefully receive it. AND you will be attracting into your own life others who will generously love and acknowledge you too.

People try too hard to be clever and snarky - to seem witty as if that will impress others and make them more memorable. It works too - they remember that they don't like you or want to be around you. And the snarky one goes to bed at night with a head full of snarky clever poisonous thoughts running around in their own head. I've found that most of the people who think they are saying something funny to me are actually saying something slightly insulting, a kind of put-down, so I avoid them in the future and they seem to wonder why I walk away when I see them coming. It's simple. <u>When you love yourself, you go where the love is and you avoid people who are withholding or snarky toward you</u>.

One of the main problems with life is that people tend to complain loudly and publicly, while appreciating and acknowledging privately and even silently. We must reverse this if we want to live a thriving life of joyous love. For some of you this will be quite out of character and therefore MORE important than almost anything else we've learned in boot camp. Make a game of it - see how many people you can GENUINELY and truthfully acknowledge, praise, bless, lift up, encourage and compliment in a day. You may be surprised how uplifted YOU will feel at the end of the day!

Day 84 – Cast Your Cares

There is an unnecessary stress that comes from taking a whole world on your shoulders. I see it as people walk into my classes, their heads filled with thoughts, thoughts, thoughts about DOING, DOING, DOING. And much of that doing has very little to do with the actions of self-love but has more to do with making things happen, preventing things from happening, planning the future or ruminating on the past.

In the opening guided meditation I help them let all that go and by the end of the 20-minute process they are all soft and open, like puppies waking up from a nice nap. The secret of manifestation is that the more relaxed and open we are, the clearer the path is to our greater good. We light up on the Universal Radar and we can easily be found by the dreams that we've been dreaming. Stress and tension constricts the valve through which our good flows.

Remember every day to cast your cares on the Divine Presence that keeps planets revolving around the sun, turning seeds into flowers, and embryos into babies. You cannot do everything yourself and it is self-tyranny to try.

Day 85 – Your Horrible Secret Shame . . .

Is probably not the big deal that you think it is. One of the few gifts of years of daytime talk shows full over over-sharing is that virtually anything that's happened so far in your life has been talked about on national television at one time or another. And no matter how horrific the experience was or is that you may feel embarrassed about, you are not alone. Still, as "out there" as we think everything is these days, there is still a virulently strong puritanical uptight vibe that runs through the fabric of America which keeps far too many people feeling like damaged goods. It's bullshit.

You don't have to go on national television or take to the Internet to bring everything out in the open unless you really feel strongly that it would be helpful to you. But you also don't need to go through life feeling like there is a scarlet A on your chest because of your multiple bankruptcies or hoarding problem or genital herpes or having a child at 14 you gave up to adoption or that you never graduated from high school or that you have a lot of very mean thoughts about your family or that you were raped or molested or that you lied to get into college or not being there when your wife passed away or some part of the body that isn't "normal" or having been fired or a million other endless scenarios. And the amazing thing is that sometimes the very minor issues will stop a person from fully living their lives while some major challenge will just be the grist for the mill of another. It's not what's happened in our lives, it's what we then make of what's happened that stops us in our tracks forever - or becomes the thing that spurs us on to a deeper life.

Because of the work I do and perhaps because of my personality, people have been telling me their deep dark secrets since I was a small child. I cannot tell you how many times over the years someone has come to me and told me a story that they thought was the most TERRIBLE thing anyone has ever admitted out loud, only to have me honestly reply, *"Hmmm, sounds like a typical human life to me. Nothing shocking or surprising here. Keep it moving."*

Horrible things happen in this world, all the time actually and few of us get out unscathed one way or another. And we also tend to make our share of mistakes along the way. If we let these be the reasons that we withhold full glorious self-love from ourselves . . . well, I am quite sure that NO ONE of the planet would love themselves. Do NOT let the beliefs of the Victorian undercurrent of this culture keep you in the shadows of guilt and shame. Your horrible secret shame is most likely shared by millions of others who are wonderful lovable people - just like you.

DAY 86 – PATIENCE, PATIENCE

Patience is one of those things that is usually under the category of easier said than done for some of us. However, it is a real expression of self-love to learn patience - mostly because the lack of it is so very bad for us.

And really, it's much more than patience regarding the big things in life that you may want. Practicing patience in traffic, in line, with people who are not moving or talking or living at the speed that we think of as normal - well, it does us a world of good when we can make progress with this every day kind of patience.

More than that, our patience with others is also reflected in our patience with ourselves. If we can give the other person a break, it's much easier to give ourselves that same break. It is our self-imposed perfectionism that allows us to so easily project it onto the poor stranger standing or driving in front of us. So in the end, thought it may seem like we are practicing patience in order to be kinder to others, WE are the ones who ultimately benefit in so many ways, including lower blood pressure, less acidic stomach problems and a more serene state of mind as we move through our days, which usually means a more peaceful night's sleep. What we think we are doing for others usually ends up doing us as much good as it does them, if not more. So try practicing patience with others and the world as an exercise in self-love and care. Watch what happens.

Day 87 – Watch Your Attitude

As you learn to practice self-love more and more, as you find this love growing and expanding within you, you will probably also find some other things decreasing and dissolving. Defensiveness and the endless need to correct others will usually start to fade away as you become more comfortable with yourself and your own truth. This "live and let live" attitude will bring you an enormous amount of inner peace and contentment - and it will increase the amount of harmony in your relationships. However, we may also find at times that when we become a little more disciplined within ourselves, we can allow ourselves to become more aware of and intolerant of those who we feel are not so disciplined. This is a HUGE mistake that will bring nothing but pain and misery.

When we have a bad attitude, it is a reflection of a mental state that is the extreme opposite of gratitude and appreciation. The most positive and powerful mental state we can have is of gratitude and appreciation for what is. Forever being dissatisfied and finding fault with others or with situations or with the world is a vibration that eats away at the host. Now that you are so close to the end of boot camp it can be tempting to get a cocky attitude rather than simply one of pride in accomplishment. You should be proud of all the growth you've gone through, for sticking with it, for challenging yourself and learning from mistakes along the way. The mistake would be to start looking around and thinking that you now know what everyone else "should" be doing or not doing.

The fastest way to neutralize any kind of a bad attitude is not through demeaning and berating yourself (which many of us erroneously thought) but rather to amp up our gratitude and appreciation for everyone and everything. Look for the good in people and situations every day as a simple exercise in keeping a good attitude. Remember that when all other things are equal, attitude is the "difference maker" in life. More people lose jobs and opportunities over a bad attitude than over lack of skills or experience. I'm not talking about putting on a "nice" act at work either. Attitude is more than what you say or do - people can SMELL it on you, they FEEL it even if your behavior doesn't reflect it. Attitude is often the difference between success and failure in life.

DAY 88 – TAKE A BOW

Or a victory lap, or whatever you want to call it when you simply receive the positive energy that is coming at you whether it is a crowd applauding or having a few friends sing happy birthday to you. Let it in. Receive it fully. Don't rush out of the spotlight out of embarrassment. It's an energetic love vibe that is coming your way and you deserve it.

When you get comfortable with receiving the loving attention of others, it's a good sign that you are loving yourself more. You no longer NEED or crave the attention, but you can let it in and enjoy it in a balanced and joyous way. It's a two-way energetic vibe of loving enthusiasm that goes back and forth between the giver and receiver.

Think of the thrill you feel applauding your favorite live band or performer, or how much joy there is in watching a loved one gleefully open a gift that you carefully picked out because you knew they would love it. Giving and receiving are two sides of the love coin, like inhaling and exhaling. Enjoy it all.

DAY 89 – FAKE IT TIL YOU MAKE IT

Well Soldier of Light, tomorrow is boot camp graduation day. You've come a very long way and made some amazing and major shifts in your Consciousness - some of them you are not even aware of yet. What you've learned here must not be discarded and forgotten now while you just go back to the old way of doing tings. It's all been leading up to a new vista, a way of living in which what is happening on the outside is no longer the determiner of your self-perception.

However, this doesn't mean there won't be backsliding and challenges along the path. The main thing is, you are prepared for them now even if you won't always know exactly what to DO in every situation. I certainly don't, but I am more sure-footed than ever before. And here's a little trick for your self-love toolbox to keep handy. It's the tried and true *"fake it til you make it."* And all this means is that there are times when rather than falling into an old negative mental habit of self criticism and doubt . . . well, you can at the very least PRETEND that you love yourself and "act the part" to see if you can just prime the pump. Rather than going back to some old self-sabotaging behavior, think of what you might do if you DID love yourself right now, and do that. It's a way of taking actions that fool us into actually FEELING differently. It's not a long-term solution, but it can be extremely powerful to shift you into a higher vibration and mental state until you are on more solid ground. An excellent tool for your kit.

DAY 90 – CONGRATULATIONS SOLDIER!

You are so amazing. You made it all the way through and I salute you for your willingness and courage to walk this path with us. I encourage you to keep on encouraging yourself, championing yourself, and being on your own team for all the days and nights of your life. You are a soldier of self-lovology now and are ready to go out as a Light to the world sharing the joy of inner-peace and self-acceptance.

This is not love based on being perfect - it is loved based on acceptance of yourself just the way you are, and just the way you are not. You will continue to change and learn and grow to be more authentically yourself, exploring the romance of a lifetime. The world is a more beautiful and safer place with you in it now because you are one of the ones who have already found what you were looking for - you are not a starving beggar at the gate, but a self-reliant giver and receiver of the love, peace and joy of the Universe. I am so proud of you! Thank you for showing up for yourself in this way and inspiring us all. May your Light shine brightly and brilliantly all through this life and beyond.

ABOUT JACOB GLASS

Jacob Glass has been teaching successfully throughout Southern California for over 30 years and is a highly sought after speaker and Consciousness Coach. This is his seventh published book. If you want to learn more about Jacob or receive his weekly class recordings or support materials please see his website jacobglass.com.

CPSIA information can be obtained
at www.ICGtesting.com
Printed in the USA
FSOW02n1100170116
15884FS